The Velvet Rope

Ayanna Dozier

BLOOMSBURY ACADEMIC
NEW YORK • LONDON • OXFORD • NEW DELHI • SYDNEY

BLOOMSBURY ACADEMIC
Bloomsbury Publishing Inc
1385 Broadway, New York, NY 10018, USA
50 Bedford Square, London, WC1B 3DP, UK

BLOOMSBURY, BLOOMSBURY ACADEMIC and the Diana logo are trademarks of
Bloomsbury Publishing Plc

First published in the United States of America 2020

Library of Congress Cataloging-in-Publication Data
Names: Dozier, Ayanna, author.
Title: The velvet rope / Ayanna Dozier.
Description: New York: Bloomsbury Academic, 2020. | Series: 33 1/3; 148 |
Includes bibliographical references. | Summary: "Discusses a pivitol
album in Janet Jackson's career through the lense of black feminist
poetics" – Provided by publisher.
Identifiers: LCCN 2020009106 | ISBN 9781501355028 (paperback) | ISBN
9781501355042 (pdf) | ISBN 9781501355035 (ebook)
Subjects: LCSH: Jackson, Janet, 1966-. Velvet rope. | Feminism and music.
Classification: LCC ML420.J153 D69 2020 | DDC 782.42166092–dc23
LC record available at https://lccn.loc.gov/2020009106

ISBN: PB: 978-1-5013-5502-8
ePDF: 978-1-5013-5504-2
eBook: 978-1-5013-5503-5

Series: 33⅓

Typeset by Deanta Global Publishing Services, Chennai, India
Printed and bound in the United States of America

To find out more about our authors and books visit www.bloomsbury.com and sign
up for our newsletters.

Contents

Track Listing

1. "Interlude – Twisted Elegance" (0:42)
2. "Velvet Rope" (4:55)
3. "You" (4:42)
4. "Got 'Til It's Gone" (4:01)
5. "Interlude – Speaker Phone" (0:54)
6. "My Need" (3:44)
7. "Interlude – Fasten Your Seatbelts" (0:19)
8. "Go Deep" (4:42)
9. "Free Xone" (4:57)
10. "Interlude – Memory" (0:04)
11. "Together Again" (5:01)
12. "Interlude – Online" (0:19)
13. "Empty" (4:32)
14. "Interlude – Full" (0:12)
15. "What About" (4:24)
16. "Every Time" (4:17)
17. "Tonight's The Night" (5:07)

Acknowledgments

I would like to extend my deepest gratitude to Leah Babb-Rosenfeld, Amy Martin, and the rest of the wonderful editorial and administrative team at Bloomsbury for working with me on this project and for the opportunity to put pen to paper (or finger to keyboard?). I am extremely grateful for Sean Maloney's generous and astute editorial feedback. Thanks to Autumn Knight and Coleman Collins for your invaluable insight pertaining to the structure and form of the chapters. A special thank you to Teo Blake for your input and for allowing me to rabidly discuss this project with you at length over various talks, drafts, and edits of this book. Special thanks to all of my colleagues, advisers (Dr. Alanna Thain and Dr. Carrie Rentschler), my sister Diana and her family and my friends who had to hear me tirelessly discuss this project over the past year, but especially Sarah Maldonado (I am your belayer!). And finally, thank you to Janet Jackson, Jimmy Jam, and Terry Lewis for *The Velvet Rope*, a work that inspires me to speak, still.

Preface

"Oh, so you one of them angry bitches, huh? A feminist."
—Lucky to Justice, *Poetic Justice*

I learned about feminism from Janet Jackson. Or, rather, through Janet Jackson's character in John Singleton's *Poetic Justice* (1993) at the age of four. I was transfixed by Janet's portrayal of Justice. She was a writer who spoke freely. Justice demanded respect and to be treated with dignity, a simple request that often is not delivered to Black women in society. If Justice's declaration for respect rendered her angry and "bitchy," it meant she was also a feminist. Her feminism came not from a "unified" position of womanhood but, rather, was informed by her position of being a Black woman in the world. She retorts, "Listen, I'm a Black woman, okay? I deserve respect. Don't you be calling me no bitch." To hear a Black woman name her self-worth in a position of being a Black woman set my mind aflame. During my next trip to the public library, I grabbed the encyclopedia for *F* and looked up *feminism*. And, my life has been made all the better for it.

I did not grow up in a feminist household. While my single mother exhibited strength, courage, and defiance in the face of oppression due to her race, gender, and class, she is thoroughly not a feminist. She taught her children what many women do: to internalize self-hatred for oneself, to prioritize the affection and attention of men (no matter the harm those men may bring), and to remain silent about your oppression and the oppression of others, mainly women, around you. I did not learn to "speak out" from *Poetic Justice*, but I learned to recognize that the world and home I lived in did not value my voice. For most of my own growth as a woman, I can point to the work of Janet Jackson in providing me a template of learning how to express myself in environments that do not want to hear the words I have to say. *The Velvet Rope*, however, is an album that spearheaded my desire to speak critically about my worldview.

This book is not about me. It *is* about mapping out Janet's journey toward emancipation through self-actualization in *The Velvet Rope*. Self-actualization refers to the fulfillments of one's potential. I appear here and there as *The Velvet Rope* has been, and remains, a critical document for my own ongoing road toward self-actualization. I largely refer to Ms. Jackson as Janet throughout the book to center her artistic license and creative control, and to retain her autonomy as a solo artist outside of her iconic family's last name. Moreover, I would like to signal here that this book is a Black feminist project—I pay close attention to how Janet's road to self-actualization carries political possibilities and emancipatory potential for all people but specifically Black women. Imaging emancipation from oppression is *The Velvet Rope*'s endgame. As such, the chapters and songs discussed in this book are organized thematically, tracing Janet's arc from from pain to liberation.

The words of Afro-Cuban philosopher Sylvia Wynter may be useful here: "How can one fly in the face of a reality, even where one is condemned by, and in, it?" These words speak to the very real oppressive structures in place that wield and enact power against bodies at the margins in society due to their race, class, gender, and sexuality—bodies that are condemned to live without the right to *a life*.[1] There is no one answer in Wynter's work that points to a solution. However, Wynter affirms the power of narrative from those condemned bodies in inspiring new ways of living freely in the world through the production of art. *The Velvet Rope* gave me the possibility of imagining what living freely might look like and what *words* that possibility of living freely might take. These words appear here and so does *The Velvet Rope*.

1
A Special Need

The more I listened to their recorded performances—of
songs composed both by the artists themselves and by
others—the more I realized that their music could serve
as a rich terrain for examining a historical feminist
consciousness that reflected the lives of working-class Black
communities.[1]
—*Angela Davis*

"I've never seen Janet so . . . Black!" my mother proclaimed
upon viewing Janet Jackson's video for "Got 'Til It's Gone."
The multiple bare-faced "Janets" danced on the screens
in Sam Goody at our local mall, The Galleria at Tyler in
Riverside, California. I had just turned seven, and my
mother reluctantly allowed me to drag her into the store.
As much I loved music, my age and religiously conservative
Black household limited my engagement with the world.
Alternative music did not make its way indoors, at least not
until I was twelve. My mother allowed me to drag her into
that Sam Goody *because* it was Janet Jackson and most Black
conservative households carry some perceived allegiance

to the Jackson family. But, she was not expecting, nor was she comfortable with, the Janet that expressed herself in that video *or* on the album. My mother's bewilderment and my excitement came from the fact that in all of the previous Janet eras, *The Velvet Rope* was the first to showcase Janet at her most different, experimental, and *Black*.

The first video for *The Velvet Rope* was set in a club lounge in apartheid South Africa and was Janet's first video to *exclusively* feature Black people. "Got 'Til It's Gone," included an appearance and rap by Q-Tip and the legendary Joni Mitchell, who remains largely unseen in the video. Janet wore her natural hair for the video in several extended and upright twist-outs covering the crown of her head. The video's cinematography captures the luminous potential of varying shades of Black skin to soak up light, sweat, water—to not only radiate but also glisten onscreen. I had never seen Black bodies in a moving image look that resplendent, raw, and natural. "Got 'Til It's Gone" captured Black skin's potential for soaking up the lime- and moonlight. It was, and remains, one of the most dynamic visuals that I have ever encountered.

The Velvet Rope exhibited Janet's interest in working with and through Black cultural production, ushered in a more "harder" sound. Black cultural production refers to the process of making art/work in spaces and with individuals racialized as Black. Prior to *The Velvet Rope*, we all knew Janet was Black and that she came from one of the Blackest families and contributors to twentieth-century Black music. But this *Janet* was in tune with the blues, hip-hop, and funk—with the *other* side of being Black that was not the type of "respectable" Black you would be in public. Respectable attitudes in the production and performance of a racialized body advocate for uplifting the race through appearances and sound to appease Eurocentric features and production. Such a production and performance limits the visibility of Black difference. Some Black artists gained visibility by participating in the "dominant" counter-production of respectability, whether or not that counter-production applied to their lives or not. The social imagination of what Black could be was limited. *The Velvet Rope* brought an image that was not only "different" but very Black to that structure, spearheading new conversations around Black identity politics.

Emerging out of a family that participated in the Motown era, Janet's formative years inevitably were influenced by the production of Black women entertainers who presented a "respectable, acceptable" portrayal of Black femininity. Respectability politics refer to the self and communal management of Black individual's social behavior, believing that presentation of the "well-behaved" would usher forth equitable treatment of Black people in the United States. Scholar Lisa B. Thompson writes of this history as the tension between the "circulating ideologies such as the Cult of True Womanhood and the Cult of Domesticity, which emphasized piety, purity, and submissiveness, held promise for revising notions about Black people as immoral."[2] Thus, there is an overwhelming focus on Black women's bodies as a representative of the race and a deep belief that changing the appearance of Black women through the adoption of respectable qualities would uplift the race and counter those notions of "immoral" behavior.

In her book *On Racial Icons*, Nicole Fleetwood writes that internal image makers at Motown like Maxine Powell trained and molded entertainers to be the "epitome of upwardly mobile, adult bourgeois charm . . . one that refuted notions of Black excess."[3] This is not to say that the earlier versions of Janet seen on *Control*, *Rhythm Nation 1814*, and *janet.* followed this aforementioned practice pushed forth through the Motown system, but they were visuals that bridged the gap for mainstream white audiences to accept Janet as a pop star in the late 1980s and early 1990s.

Janet's dominance in the media prior to *The Velvet Rope* was one situated on refuting practices of Black excess, be that in sound or image. This Janet had no fucks to give, conveying her woes through her aesthetics, purposefully deploying citations that were produced by Black culture—natural hair, symbols from the ancestral African tribe of the Akan—and working with emerging hip-hop artists. *The Velvet Rope* was personal, but the specific Afro-diasporic citation was Janet's way of linking her personal struggles with shared diasporic political struggles of other Black women. That is what made *The Velvet Rope* Janet so Black in my mother's eyes. We walked out of Sam Goody that day with a CD of *The Velvet Rope* (which I am still baffled that she bought) and a new image of Janet—one with "defiant" hair, piercings, tattoos, different, and very *Black*. It is an image that I have latched on to from that moment on.

Downright Mean

The press were anticipating Janet's sixth studio album before the production of *The Velvet Rope* began. Following the completion of her RCA contract, Janet signed a one-album contract with Virgin for $30 million in 1992, the highest at that time.[4] After the success of *janet.* she renewed her contract with Virgin for a staggering $80 million, which remains one of the highest contractual signing for a recording artist ever.[5] To say that Janet was at the top of her career would be a gross understatement. Janet was at the top, period. *The Velvet Rope* would team Janet up, again, with longtime producing partners Jimmy Jam and Terry Lewis in addition to listing production and writing credits to her then (secret) husband Renée Elizondo Jr. for the first time. The public (and press) were startled that the next album would be Janet's "most personal" yet and would deal with her two-year battle with depression. The press's reaction was combative: How can *you* be depressed?[6] Janet, who just signed an $80 million record deal. Janet, who is one of the sexiest women in the world. Janet, who was born into one of the most famous entertainment families of all time. *You*, depressed? *I don't think so*, was the collective response.[7]

In addition, Janet found herself having to "speak" on behalf of Michael's tumultuous life. She maintained her spotlight and resented being used to gain insight on his experiences. The press read this insistence for autonomy as a rivalry.[8] When you're sixteen, growing up in the shadow of a brother crowned the King of Pop must not have made carving out an identity easy, and yet, Janet did. As a testament to the autonomy that Janet worked so hard to obtain, starting with *Control* and solidifying it with *janet.*, this book will focus on Janet's life and her worldview as retrieved from numerous interviews, writings, songs, videos, and anecdotes.

I will be neither approaching nor thoroughly considering the worldview of her siblings, specifically Michael.

I did not conduct any interviews for this book but rather approached unpacking the album and its production with available materials: interviews, media documentation, reviews, music videos, and, of course, the album itself. I look at the album for its conceptual properties and metaphors to narrate Janet's process toward self-actualization. I work with the given properties of the text and expand upon them by bringing historical and theoretical positions that may help clarify or contextualize Janet's voice, the response, or incidents surrounding the album, which include an unfortunate wealth of media backlash.

The apprehension facing *The Velvet Rope* began to rise as Janet started the promotional tour for the album. *The Velvet Rope* is about the need to reconcile with the past, utilizing metaphors around barriers, inclusion, and bondage. Male reviewers were explicitly disinterested in the album's narrative arc. One of the few interviews where Janet received sensitivity to the album's content on abuse and neglect came from her interview with Laura B. Randolph for *Ebony* magazine—a stark contrast to other reviewers who felt that Janet manufactured pain to sell records.[9]

The interviews and a large majority of the reviews for the album are emblematic of racialized sexism delivered in print. The "bad" press stemmed from men not wanting to affirm women's issues because to do so would have them address how they are complicit, benefit from, and potentially enable the oppression of women in society. *The Velvet Rope* was met with "mixed" reviews and attention placed not on what was being said but on her body and her fluctuating weight. In his *Rolling Stone* interview with Janet for *The Velvet Rope*, David Ritz notes, "She got her ass kicked. Her metaphors were misunderstood. Word was she was into bondage. Or she was depressed. They said the album wasn't selling. They said the tour was bombing. The press was hostile and, for the first time in Janet's career, downright mean."[10]

Many reviewers felt frustrated by Janet's "poeticism." The suggestion was that if this was her most "personal" album, why wasn't she "telling" us everything? Such an inquiry is troubling for it places an onus on women to testify their pain in order to be believed. It is not enough to state that you are a victim; we need to know the details and demand that you relive and re-perform that trauma. The problem with the testimony is that it operates under a system that will use your words against you.

The constant need for women to testify their pain, Black women especially, articulates the performance dynamic of the testimony and the fact that performing pain incited by racial or sexual abuse, historically, has been a place of pleasure for others in the United States. I can imagine that Janet's insistence on ambiguity at times was a foresight of self-preservation. In a BBC "making of" featurette for "I Get Lonely," she stated the following, "I've lost a lot of privacy. I don't believe in giving it all up."[11] The need to keep some things to herself was a way to not fully participate in the sharing economy that often demands women re-perform their abuse on demand. *The Velvet Rope*, yes, features Janet at her most vulnerable, her most personal, but also at her most in control regarding the form her "testimony" was going to take.

Aesthetics

The album cover shows Janet's roots. Literally. The bulk of Ellen von Unwerth's portrait of Janet is made up of her hennaed red tresses as she casts her head down, eyes closed, wearing a black long-sleeve shirt against a burgundy backdrop. The portrait is markedly different from *janet.*'s assertive gaze toward the viewer, with her hands resting upon her mane of curls, coyly smirking at her audience. The Janet on the cover of *janet.* was hiding something in the truncated image that would be revealed in the September 1993 issue of *Rolling Stone* that showed a bare-breasted Janet wearing jeans with the hands of her then husband and artistic collaborator, Renée Elizondo Jr., covering her nipples. *The Velvet Rope*'s packaging and production design was by Len Peltier, Steve Gerdes, and Flavía Cureteu. Interior photography was produced by both Ellen von Unwerth and Mario Testino, with additional tour and promotional singles photography by Renée Elizondo Jr.

If *janet.* was her "sexual" debut, then *The Velvet Rope* was her rebellious one. Janet unveiled a physical transformation to match her internal rebellion, which included a series of piercings (septum, nipple, and labia). Her natural hair in tight red curls, a departure from the looser curl pattern audiences grew to associate with her image. Her attire consisted of low-cut black blazers, trousers, bustiers, and the occasional turtleneck, in addition to several visible tattoos—most notably the Sankofa symbol from the Akan culture (located in present-day Ghana) on her right wrist. These liner notes photographs demonstrate that Janet, although melancholic, was not interested in losing the sexual freedom and the need "to accept [her]self as a woman and express [her]self as an artist."[12] Like *Rhythm Nation 1814* before it, the aesthetics of the album were visual extensions of the themes expressed and heard in the songs.

The same "gravity-defying" twist-outs that appeared in the "Got 'Til It's Gone" video were styled for the bulk of Janet's European and Australian promotional tour, causing quite the spectacle. When prompted by a French reporter to "explain" the style, Janet declared that "I just wanted to go back to what I used to see when I was a kid. I would see all the neighborhood kids wear their hair like this and in different braids and I always thought it was so cool."[13] For her appearance on the Australian broadcast *Hey Hey*, the interviewer and predominantly white audience gasped when Janet revealed that she spends upward of thirty-five minutes to achieve that look.[14] On the red carpet for the VH1 Fashion Awards in 1998, Janet, now rocking her near Black loose curls, recalled the interest in her hair and style choices for *The Velvet Rope* promotional tour with some irritation, "They had a lot of commentary about that look in Europe. A Lot!"[15]

Even in 1997, mainstream Western media had a deep aversion to representing Black women with their natural hair and/or in natural hairstyles, opting instead to overrepresent Black women with straight hair or loose tresses. And while the natural hair movement has gained popularity/ visibility through social media today, there is still a wealth of discrimination around Black women's natural hair texture and hairstyles. Scholar Cheryl Thompson argues that Eurocentric values of "straight, long, and flowing hair has a sociocultural effect on Black women's notions of physical attractiveness, but also on courtship, self-esteem, and identity."[16] This is to say that Janet's hair during *The Velvet Rope* era not only challenged representations of her beauty that she produced within her career prior to that album but also served as a representational counter-production to a "negative obsession" of natural hair.[17] Janet's interviews support Thompson's argument. When speaking with Oprah, she said that her desire as a child to have dreadlocks, tattoos, and piercings was never fulfilled because she was not allowed to have them; it was only through the album, she said, that she was finally able to do whatever she wanted with her body, including her hair.[18]

The Sankofa symbol became a motif throughout the album's packaging as well as the tour. The symbol originates from a variety of Gold Coast African tribes prior to and during the trans-Atlantic slave trade. The symbol used for *The Velvet Rope* emerges from the Akan tribe. In Yoruba mythology and culture (originated in Nigeria and practiced widely in the Caribbean and Americas), Sankofa refers to an engagement with remembrance; to move forward, one must deal with their past. Janet's invocation of memory on and in *The Velvet Rope* exists both on the level of the personal and in the realm of the public. Janet ties an Afro-diasporic remembrance symbol to hold onto memory as a way of making memory fluid and not petrifying it to time.

Visually, Janet was determined to reconcile with herself through self-acceptance/actualization. Those personal issues that she was struggling with around body image were also rooted in her self-acceptance as a Black woman against the overwhelming Eurocentrism and Black respectability that dominates and dictates Black women's representation. *The Velvet Rope*'s visuals and aesthetics are lauded in 2020 but risked alienation of Janet's mainstream fans at the time. She writes in *True You* (her 2011 memoir-esque self-help book) that she recognized the comparisons made between her body and non-Black bodies were unfair and that she "had internalized those comparisons and on some level had actually been traumatized by them. I wanted to be free of all that."[19] Liberation for Janet meant centering Black cultural modes of beauty production, and that was deemed a colossal risk—for Black liberation is perceived threatening or risky in whatever form it takes.

Twisted Elegance

The Velvet Rope begins with an intervening period of time— an interlude, "Twisted Elegance." What is the elegance that Janet is referring to and why is it twisted? My mother was a seamstress so I always conjured up an image of a woman crafting a lavish garment upon hearing those words. The product may be some dark fantasy, but the crafting of it, the process, was chaos. Sewing is messy business. So is musical production. Scraps of paper everywhere, scraps of fabric on the ground, scraps of memory haunting, and shadowing the production of the final product: a product, an album that would be labeled as Janet's "dark masterpiece."[20] Elegant in its final form, the aesthetic crafting of *The Velvet Rope* was twisted and painful. "Twisted Elegance" sheds some insight into the aesthetics of the album that will shape how Janet reveals and conceals a narrative of her personal woes and desires.

Janet's last album to label an "interlude" was *Rhythm Nation 1814*. (On *janet.*, the interludes are embedded as tracks.) In signposting the interludes, Janet suggests that *The Velvet Rope* will carry structural similarities, and critiques, to *Rhythm Nation 1814* but also that the nondescript passage of time is a critical listening strategy. If *Rhythm Nation 1814* used the interlude to argue against the cyclical nature of oppression then the interlude, here, may be used to examine memory's capacity for repetition no matter how painful that memory is. Janet states over changing radio channel static the following passage: "It's my belief that we all have the need to feel special/ And it's this need that can bring out the best of us, yet the worst of us." In these few short words, Janet announced her need to feel "special" and the narrative arc that would dictate the rest of the album.

The interlude provides an auditory reprieve for listeners in between songs and at the same time allows listeners to gain insights into the flow and meaning of the album. Interludes have long had a tradition in Black cultural production as a device to introduce drama, narrative arc, role play, and critique in the space of the album where such dramaturgical exercises may not be available to Black musicians in abundance. Janet's use of the interlude was never meant to be just a pause between songs but rather a way to produce a social landscape within the span of seconds. Over the course of *The Velvet Rope*, the interludes would be used to further Janet's interest in narration by providing vignettes for songs, in addition to capturing how we *live* and *feel* in the late twentieth century. The former can be heard on interludes like "Fasten Your Seatbelts" for the song "Go Deep," whereas the latter example can be heard in the interlude "Online," which features the sound of an internet dial-up modem. Lastly, Janet uses the interlude as a space for poetry featured with "Interlude: Twisted Elegance," "Interlude: Full," and "Interlude: Sad." *The Velvet Rope* feels more immersive because of her rich and, at times, experimental use of interludes that suggest a process of world building through auditory production.

Emerging from the nineteenth-century Black folklore literary traditions, Black women learned to adapt and experiment with forms of narration that do not always announce their stories in "linear," tangible forms. These plurisignant texts utilized different narrative strategies to complicate, refuse, and blur the narrative structure of the characters involved, giving way to ambiguity rather than absolute resolution. We may want to view Black women's *narrative experimentation* in music, for example, as similarly producing a productive avenue to subvert audience response and to deliver accounts that lack representation otherwise.[21]

Black women have always been the vanguard of Black musical production, especially when it comes to singing the blues, where, as Davis states above, they were able to sing through their Black working-class consciousness. What is unique about the sonic interventions of Black women is how they articulate their "truths" not just lyrically but through a pluri-conceptual practice that includes vocality, narrative, and the use of interludes. If Black women's voices are routinely policed in society then the breaths, screams, pants, runs, cries, coos, and suspended engagements with time serve as key explorations of Black women's consciousness that largely remain under-examined in Black culture politics and its histories. It is this aesthetic practice that Janet placed herself in dialogue with in order to weave the sonic landscape of personal woes, sexual affirmation, reconciliation, and emancipation from oppressive thought and practice in *The Velvet Rope*. The aesthetics of the narrative are their own form of twisted elegance dictating the seams of the album's construction and the listener's engagement.

2
Like the Blues Need the Pain

> To Sing the blues the writer must be haunted by the same
> sickness; and the same wound. Our wounds must haunt
> us, in our exile in the invisible nation, every minute of our
> waking day. If we don't sing the blues for our own pain, who
> will sing the blues for them?[1]
> —*Sylvia Wynter*

"Velvet Rope"

The first note we hear is distortion. The distortion is followed by a cascading flow of amplifying timbres and frequencies produced by electronic amps and instruments. The flow stops. We then hear a sonic contrast to the cacophony, a series of ever so subtle strings. The sounds paint an image of a sinner running from the night, stepping into the church to hear heaven's gate beckon upon their entry. Janet's airy voice invites us beyond her velvet rope by declaring that "We have a special need/ to feel that we belong." Upon the second iteration of the chorus line, a metronomic beat provides stability—a ground to stand on before Jam, Lewis, and Jackson bless us with one of the best examples of a sample: Malcom McLaren and the World Famous Supreme Team's "The Hobo Scratch." What makes the inclusion of the "Hobo Scratch" so unique (different from its use in Beyoncé's 2003 B-side, "Sexuality") is the layering of another sample, Mike Oldfield's 1973 album-long track, "Tubular Bells." The combination of the funk-punk conveyed in "The Hobo Scratch" is rendered oddly dis-familiar from the climbing guitars and bagpipes that make up "Tubular Bells."

The truncated version of "Tubular Bells" used for *The Exorcist* (1973) is the sampled version for "Velvet Rope." Thematically, "Velvet Rope" speaks about inclusion and an attempt to abolish the divide that keeps individuals on the other side of the velvet rope. Be those societal "velvet ropes" or the internal ones that hinder self-examination and emancipation. If Janet's voice is a heavenly invitation inside, then *The Exorcist* sample may have also been a strategic one in alerting listeners of a young girl, in this case a woman, literally in need of exorcising her demons.

Lyrically, the song is straightforward and on the surface does not add any "insight" into the singer's psyche. However, the lyrics are conceptually rich metaphors, especially when paired with the sonic manipulations and overall composition of the song. At one point, Janet refers to a habit of putting others down as a way to uplift oneself and that oppressing her will ultimately oppress themselves in the process. Janet also declares that judgment and hate exist outside of her velvet rope. This statement becomes richer when read in the larger context of a need to unlearn a conservative, respectable position that she inherited from her family. A process of unlearning that demands a move toward openness and toward a Black feminist political affirmation of one's being and their personal woes. The "Velvet Rope" sets up the album's long arc toward emancipation of one's consciousness.

The song crescendoes to a violin solo from Singaporean, British artist Vanessa Mae during its bridge. The experimental use of the violin on the track will always be a standout use of genre-mixing. A journalist for *Vibe* magazine, however, was less convinced by the pain expressed on *The Velvet Rope* "and its bland ass title song."[2] What was missing from the reviewer was a desire to participate. "Velvet Rope" only works if you join the ride and want to believe Janet's journey and maintain an open engagement with experimentation. "Velvet Rope" carries different instruments, samples, and sounds that are forcibly merged together to create an uneasy tension. It works, but barely. The opening track fine-tunes the listener's ears to expect something different from Janet, a sound that was decidedly not pop and certainly was not there to appease limited perspectives of the singer.

Black Feminist Blues Politics

"My siblings and I grew up with the belief that you don't let people know what is going on inside. We didn't carry our problems onstage. Fans paid hard-earned money to watch us perform, and our job was to make them happy. End of story."[3] Janet's familial habit of burying one's emotions for the sake of the audience may have also been shaped by the overwhelming archive of media images that paint the expression of emotions by Black individuals as extreme or "uncivilized." As Janet would later detail in *True You*, the need to suppress her emotions extended itself beyond the perimeters of the stage and was a practice that dictated her relationships with others. Burying your emotions already suggests an agreement, however subliminal, with a limited, conservative perspective around what type of Black visibility is appropriate in and for society.

Black feminist theorist bell hooks reminds us that the brutal backlash to Anita Hill's testimony against Justice Clarence Thomas by Black individuals was not a "new" conservative position but, rather, one that is concomitant with Black identity formation emerging after the abolition of slavery.[4] Black respectability—which comes from this conservative position—represents itself through negation. Do *not* express your emotions. Do *not* announce your woes. *And*, condemn those Black women who speak out about their problems and counter *your* negation. Black respectability is intimately tied with a dissent to radical positions of Black liberation. Upholding a respectable position affirms to a larger audience that the stereotypes are "true," but that *this* performance of a Black body is different to *outsider* eyes. Again, bell hooks delivers the evidence of this performance from a *New York Magazine* journalist who praised the respectable, conservative positions performed by Black individuals across the nation during the Anita Hill hearings, "the nation was treated to a parade of blacks

LIKE THE BLUES NEED THE PAIN

who—for once—weren't crack dealers, athletes, welfare mothers, or any of the other stereotypes but solid citizens, fine friends, and excellent character witnesses."[5]

Politically, Janet needed to reconcile with the deeply conservative practice of respectability that was so ingrained in her childhood upbringing and enacted by her parents, siblings, and extended family members. In a 2009 interview with *Good Morning America's* Robin Roberts, Janet spoke frankly about the culture of repression and respectability that was bestowed upon her and her siblings by their parents. She remarked that she never dealt with the fact that from a young age she was forced to call her father, Joe—suggesting that the professionalized nature of her childhood and all the demands that come with being "professional" hindered her ability to express herself in any way.[6] Janet began to work through Joe's dominance and neglect for the family's emotional/personal needs on the "Miss You Much" B-side, "You Need Me," but *The Velvet Rope* would see a continuation of her desire to deal with the effect those childhood experiences had on her psyche.

In the *Newsweek* interview for *The Velvet Rope's* promotion, she stated that her relationship with her father had not gotten better simply due to the fact that he would not let her be.[7] Creatively or otherwise, Janet grew up in an environment where her father had very specific and restricting ideas about what type of Black woman she should be in the world. Again, the strict conservative hand by Joe Jackson is not a new "representation" for Black individuals, but one that has contributed to the intra-community modes of self-policing, culture of silence, lack of affirmation to Black women's personal and structural woes.

In numerous interviews, Janet maintained that her father's strictness and her mother's proudful quiet endurance could be attributed to their "old school" nature.[8] Despite the seemingly universal nature of the term "old school," the invocation used by Janet is specific to Black culture in the United States and its familial relations emerging after slavery. "Old school" in a sentence denotes a complex choreography of male dominance against the family in domestic space as that dominance was frequently stripped away from Black men in public.

Joe Jackson was the eldest of five children born to Samuel Joseph Jackson (1893–1993) and Crystal Lee King (1907–92) in 1928 in Fountain Hill, Arkansas, while Katherine Jackson was the eldest of two born to Prince Albert (1907–95) and Martha Screws (1902–90) in Clayton, Alabama. Both Joe and Katherine Jackson's families would migrate to the Chicago area in the mid-twentieth century carrying their southern roots with them before settling in Gary, Indiana, a suburb outside of Chicago. When Janet says that her father was old school, she is referring to a Black consciousness that was deeply rooted in respectability politics. This practice created a tense demarcation of Black women's voices in the family— more often being regulated to extreme silence, a role that was often advocated by other Black women, especially within the family.

Religion may have also played a role in shaping the conservative values of the Jackson family. Devout Jehovah's Witnesses, the Jacksons maintained a strict relationship with God that impacted their dietary, social, communicative, and sexual practices. Janet's interest in West African mythologies and cultures in the album may have signaled her desire to find a more expansive relationship with "God." A relationship that "accepted" her as she was and that enabled a freedom of her body to exist in the world, something she may not have had in her childhood home and spiritual practices.

Part of what pulled me into *The Velvet Rope* was its sheer rebellion. My fascination with Janet's hair in the interviews and promotional coverage was because it was defiant in my mother's eyes. The bent of respectability demands sacrifices from Black women's bodies, and hair is the first one. *Good* and *Godly* Black women manage their hair. They try to attain and adhere to Eurocentric features whenever possible, and straightening your hair is often the first area of correction for Black women. To be clear, I am not suggesting that straightening your hair is a conservative practice for Black women but rather to demonstrate how Black respectability wields hair politics as part of its virtues.

In a 1954 editorial for the Black newspaper the *Pittsburgh Courier*, Torki Johnson urges Black women to "watch their manners" for the good of the race.[9] Many of the prominent mid-twentieth-century Black newspapers at the time (*Chicago Defender, Pittsburgh Courier*, the *New York Amsterdam News*, and the *Baltimore Afro-American*) frequently featured an editorial for Black women advocating for respectability in their behavior and appearance (which sadly, overwhelmingly included advertisements for skin whitening cream and harsh hair straightening lye). Editorials like Johnson's make clear that the "burden" of racial advancement hinged upon Black women not being a burden. It is not a stretch to suggest that Katherine Jackson not only adhered to this conservative practice but bestowed it upon her children. In the 2001 *MTV Icon* special dedicated to Janet Jackson, Katherine Jackson remarked that she did not like *Control* for she felt that it was inappropriate behavior for Janet to be expressing her opinion like *that*.[10] Like so many Black women before her, much of Katherine Jackson's life was about endurance in the face of adversity and she taught her children the same values. Part of the practice of endurance is to remain silent about your problems and to not be a burden onto others. (Janet affirms this internalization on *All For You*'s "Better Days.")

"You"

Friend and choreographer to Janet, Tina Landon remembers the sessions for *The Velvet Rope* going more or less the same as others, "No one really suspected anything was wrong." However, what Janet was not discussing outside of the studio was being mapped out into the architecture of the songs and the album. Landon recalls, "I remember the first sounds coming back from the album were hard, it had an edge that the other albums did not have."[11] Landon's comment is specific to her first listen of the second song on the album, "You." Like with "Rhythm Nation," before it, "You" shows Janet, Terry, and Jimmy's masterful ability to remix samples to the point where they are nearly beyond immediate recognition. With "Rhythm Nation," the sample was Kool and the Gang's "Thank You," and with "You," it was War's "Cisco Kid." If "Cisco Kid" was a laid-back jam about idolizing Duncan Renaldo's portrayal of a Mexican cowboy in the 1950s, "You" is the sinister blaze about facing up to your false promises and dreams. The sample is not only utilized for a narratively different song but one that is tonally different and that affects your relationship with the original. "You" follows the opening track, "Velvet Rope," as its aggressive sibling who calls for harsh truths to be told and reconciled. The song was released as the album's fifth single on September 3, 1998.

One can almost imagine the song emerging out of Janet's subconscious, forcing her to come to terms with her behavior and her consequences. Or, as others have suggested, "You" may have been Janet's way of subtly pointing her finger at her brother Michael. While that is not an argument I follow, I am interested in analyzing why interviewers were so eager to displace Janet's woes as a song to center her famous sibling—essentially turning the spotlight back onto Michael. One journalist asked Janet to explain the lyric "Check in the mirror my friend" if the song *was not* about Michael, to which Janet asked if he was "the only man with a mirror?"[12] Due to the constant suggestions that "You" was about Michael, Janet began repeatedly stating that she wished that she would have titled, "You" "Me" to explicitly reinforce that the song was about her burying past traumatic events.[13] The desire to displace Janet from her own story—be that to make it about her brother to gain insight into his life—was one form of reviewers' overwhelming desire to not actively listen to Janet's experiences in a meaningful way.

The lyrics for "You" are decisively clear, and the song is about Janet. She sings about releasing the frightened child that has dictated most of her adulthood. We can examine

"You" for Janet's need to forge an identity for herself and the difficulty of identity formation when you start to unlearn or move away from strict familial practices. Although the politics of "You" are not explicitly visible on the surface, when placed in a dialogue with a song like "Free Xone" on the album, it becomes evident that Janet is in the process of affirming herself and the struggles of others—an arc toward emancipation. She later acknowledges the escapism that she pursued to avoid confrontation (through performance or through relationships), "Does what they think of you determine your worth?" In this way, the song marks a political shift to fracture the consciousness of the singer and her listeners. Like the refrain "the personal is political," Janet is merging her internal crisis with a public political one. This is emphasized by Janet's spelling conscience backward during the bridge and closing refrain of the song.

I am struck by the chorus where Janet admits that her attempt to bury emotions and please others led her to sacrifice her own needs. This lyric is reminiscent of poet Audre Lorde's declaration that Black women routinely place themselves last when it comes to taking care of their political, personal, and sexual needs. Lorde asserts in "Sexism: An American Disease in Blackface" that "Black women have had compassion for everyone else but ourselves."[14] Lorde's argument was a rebuke to the overdetermined relationship race has to gender in black cultural political arguments. Who exactly is represented and, more importantly, *cared* for in a Black community or family? "You," in all its confrontation, is Janet's attempt to circumvent that dynamic of care, albeit in a manner that is more akin to "tough love" than anything else.

LIKE THE BLUES NEED THE PAIN

Personal Woes

To be frank, reading the male-led interviews with Janet for *The Velvet Rope* was thoroughly exhausting. The infamous *Vibe* interview opens with a rumor that the vegetarian Janet had been seen leaving KFC with buckets of chicken only to state, "One thing, I can tell you is that she is not fat."[15] The astute way in which the media overemphasizes women's weight was and continues to remain troubling. During her interview with Oprah, Oprah was able to get Janet to open up about her dietary habits by saying, "You know you can tell me because I have my issues as well," insofar as many women struggle with appearance and maintaining a healthy dietary habit in a misogynistic, fatphobic media landscape. And while Oprah did ask Janet point blank if she was ever bulimic, to which Janet responded in the negative, Oprah did not leave time for her to say any more about her body image struggle before moving on to the next "pressing" issue: sex—a missed opportunity that could have provided a meaningful engagement with body dysmorphia and Black women in society.

Years later in *True You*, Janet would admit that for many years she struggled with eating disorders (like abusing laxatives) during times in which her body was at its most "svelte."[16] *True You* is partially a narrative about an entertainer's life and partly about a woman still working out body issues and weight fluctuations. In that book, Janet admits to being an emotional eater. She declared that food filled the void of comfort within her, and when it was ready, she was ready.[17] Janet's admission of her disordered eating habits holds great value for demystifying the myth that Black girls and women do not have eating disorders. I look back at those interviews and even Oprah's questions and quips and recognize the very real harm that is conducted against Black women by over emphasizing their curves without positive affirmation (Janet was routinely teased and called "Booty" by her family), mocking the desire to be "thin", and not acknowledging the fraught relationship with food many Black families have that stem from socioeconomic status or spiritual-led practices, which may normalize disordered eating.

Much of Janet's relationship with body image and food emerged from her childhood and may have even been encouraged by her mother. While this is not to suggest that Janet's eating disorder was forced upon her, I am interested in the way in which her mother normalized disordered eating through dietary health habits, like colonics. Janet acknowledged the severity of the family's relationship with colonics, stating that her mother felt it was important to employ colonic treatments on a weekly basis. She writes, "The idea was that the bacteria and toxins that accumulate in the colon have to be flushed out. Later I would learn that many doctors disagree with this method, feeling that the body's digestive system naturally eliminates those toxins. There is a school of thought, however, that maintaining a healthy colon requires extraordinary measures. For many years, our family adopted those measures."[18] The mid- to late-twentieth-century popularity of weekly colonics has its roots in spiritual cleanses, that is, in order for the spirit to be clean the body must rid itself of toxins and undergo some sort of detoxification (colonics is often advertised as a way to detoxify the body).[19]

And while cleanses can be productive for the body, the normalization of this is what I am picking up upon, especially in this narrative of a weekly colonics. One colonic treatment is intended to give you a bowel movement nearly each hour for roughly forty-eight hours after treatment. A weekly practice of this may normalize this process and establish an equation of mental detoxification with a physical one that literally flushes your body out. For those who grow up with a poor image of themselves, the added link of constantly flushing your body to "feel better" in mind and spirit not only becomes a possibility (which was the case with Janet) but also may lead to other disordered eating habits like restricting food intake to achieve the same effect/desired feeling of "satisfaction."

As an individual who grew up in a household that normalized fasting, it was instilled upon me at a young age that my body (God's temple) was in constant need of cleansing. What I ate directly intersected with my spiritual holiness and availability for God's word, which was considered nourishment in and of itself. While there are many other factors that led to my battle with anorexia, Janet's *Velvet Rope* era interviews led me to make key connections between the familial relationship of the spiritual and its disordered eating habits that can often contribute to the production of an eating disorder.

At the time of *The Velvet Rope*'s promotional tour, there was a lack of sympathy for Black women to be vulnerable. Janet faced much opposition to her desire to speak about her pain.

Part of a Black feminist practice is to take the claims around one's lived experience with neglect and oppression seriously as so much of Black women's ability to speak is met with resistance. For her part, Janet was astute about pointing out the differences between her depression and the depression produced by economic despair. Janet had frequently stated in interviews the difficulty of acknowledging her depression amid social arguments that success negates troubles: "How could *she* possibly be depressed?"[20] Again, *The Velvet Rope* era saw Janet not as one with all of the answers but as one who was willing to work them out with the public. Janet's views on therapy were still very biased and conservative. She stated that she did not pursue seeking professional help because she did not want to appear "crazy."[21] Janet does point to the value of having a creative output to help her deal with her psyche in that "writing is therapy." And although sharing your struggle is politically useful for oneself and for others, creative outputs are not a one-size-fits-all solution for depression and trauma.

The statement the "personal is political" emerges from the way in which women began to speak out against male dominance in the home that constituted control over their autonomy, their reproductive rights, and ability to lay claim to their torment.[22] Abuse in the home was almost a guaranteed element of a woman's private life. So, when white women began to speak publicly about this during the second wave of feminist movement in the 1970s it provided a turning point in how women aspired to dislodge a patriarchal ideology from domestic union. Black women blues singers already created a rich oral tradition of speaking truth to their abuse and their pain, circumventing respectability politics from the

1920s onwards. When Janet turned pain into a poetic form she cited the sonic and literary history of Black women's political dissidence of the blues. The blues on the album are a political call for her to reconcile with the conservative respectable politics that she inherited and practised in her life; they provide Janet with the opportunity to sing directly from her wounds, as Wynter suggests in the epigraph.

"My Need"

"My Need" is a blues song in the "old school" tradition of the genre emerging with artists like Bessie Smith and Gertrude "Ma" Rainey. To our modern audience and to audiences in 1997, "My Need" was nothing more than a "sexual romp" song. However, to suggest that "My Need" is just about sex is to minimize the emotional and, frankly, painful examinations of longing described in the song. The song's explicit focus on the singer's sexual cravings participates in a larger practice of blues culture by Black women who were frank about their needs. The genesis of the blues is forged in the following decades after the abolition of slavery. Where, for the first time since the slave trade began, Black individuals—although still economically and politically disadvantaged in the New Americas—were free to pursue sex and relationships on their own terms.

Angela Davis argues that prior to the popularity of the blues, Black musical production was the spiritual.[23] With the blues occupying the juke joints, spirituals increasingly became domesticated in the space of the church as opposed to the collective public settings of its origins. The blues, then, became synonymous with the Devil's music due to its secular setting and thematic content. The blues spearheaded the way in which sex and the erotic was interwoven in the tapestry of heartache that made up Black culture.

Potentially inspired by Janet's former husband Renee Elizondo Jr., "My Need" is about longing, *no*, yearning for a lover's touch that seems to be not physically distant but emotionally disconnected from the singer. Take for instance, the lyric in the bridge of the song that compares Janet's sexual need to both conceptual histories of Black culture and trauma to ecological interrelationships on the planet, "Like the flowers need the rain/ Like the blues needs the pain." No lover can satisfy the demands that Janet is communicating. Earlier in the song, Janet expresses the immediacy of her need by guaranteeing her lover there is no need for promises and in turn, futures. In this way, Janet suggests that her need is only a temporary fix to the larger problems in her life, but it is a fix she will pursue nonetheless.

Like other blues songs, Janet is cheeky and frank about sex. She talks about feeling so tight for her lover and letting her lover know that there is no need for foreplay as she wants to get straight to the point. Expressions like these are key examples sure to arouse the listener and make them blush. "My Need" opens with several, *oohhs* and *ahhs*, alerting the listener to the sonic possibilities of Janet's sensual moans. The song's explicit sexual content is preceded by the amusing and interesting interlude "Speaker Phone" (whose content is too scandalous to detail in this chapter). The songs of blues singers like Bessie Smith ushered in a demand for sexual freedom for Black women during turmoil. "My Need" simultaneously holds unto Jackson's affirmation for sexual autonomy while musing through an existential crisis around emotional lack.

The wave of melancholy that structures "My Need" is very reminiscent of another "seemingly" love/sexy song by Janet, "Twenty Foreplay" from her 1995 compilation album, *Design a Decade*. Like "My Need," the song masks its pain with sex but a closer inspection of the lyrics reveals a soulful Janet using her autonomy of sex to connect to a lover and potentially run away from painful memories. To further solidify "My Need"'s relationship with the blues— and to connect to its radical potential as a Black feminist song rooted in pain yet maintaining autonomy for sexual desire—"My Need" samples both Diana Ross's mournful and moanful disco anthem "Love Hangover" and Tammi Terrell and Marvin Gaye's "You're All I Need to Get By." While these samples are rhythm-specific, lyrically and tonally the songs are in the same family.

Janet samples some of the blues' most acclaimed offspring, Motown, a style that was embodied by her elder siblings. In her 1976 chart-topping hit, "Love Hangover," Ross coos her way through her desire to hold onto her love malady, "If there's a cure for this/ I don't want to get over." In "You're All Need to Get By," Gaye and Terrell provide each other rocks to endure the coming storm. Jackson evokes both sentiments but subverts the outcome through her sexual frankness and unresolved ending. Janet's sexual dissatisfaction is rooted in a type of existential pain that sex only briefly allows her to escape from, but the pain remains all the same.

"What About"

I remember the first time hearing or rather seeing "What About" by Janet Jackson. She performed the song at the VH1 Fashion Awards in lieu of "Together Again." "Together Again" was the requested song for the ceremony as the producers did not want to sour the mood, a request that Janet rejected. The ceremony aired on October 27, 1998, toward the end of *The Velvet Rope* tour, promotion, and era. I did not watch the performance until a year after its airdate when VH1 replayed the awards ceremony in promotion for the 1999 Fashion Awards. Eager to watch not just the 1999 Fashion Awards ceremony but the critical 1998 Fashion Awards ceremony, I successfully managed to hot box cable from our neighbors (without their knowledge) for the re-airing, which sustained our cable access "free of charge" for the next six years.

For the uninitiated, this process involves attaching a coaxial cord splitter to someone else's main line exterior cable connection source and then running your own coaxial cord to your television set. The advent of WIFI routers/digital cable boxes has made this specific iteration of "hotboxing" more and more obsolete. Access to media was limited by a variety of intersecting social, economic, and religious structures affecting my household. Stealing my neighbor's cable for six years for me is masked with moral ambivalence. I gained insight into other ways of being, of living that were being strictly prohibited in my home. Most critically though, for Janet's VH1 performance of "What About," I saw a Black woman openly name her abuse via performance, an act that other women in my family were, sadly, not doing.

I was startled by the intense emotional display by Janet onstage, the brutality of the song matched Tina Landon's choreography pantomiming domestic abuse. The performance begins with Janet on her knees staring intensely at the camera, heaving deep breaths. The song starts. We hear the sound of waves plunging over one another as she sings about walking along the beach—the picturesque moonlight image of romantic courtship. The first verse creates a false start. The seemingly serene nature of a lover proposing marriage to the singer is torn asunder by the singer's internal thoughts. Janet rages her thoughts against an electric guitar. "What about the times you hit my face/ What about the times you said no one would want me?"

I had heard the song before, but this performance shook me to my core; it still does. Janet was doing the "unthinkable," announcing via a televised performance that she's endured abuse at the hands of a loved one. To speak out against a male member in the community in this manner can be framed as an assault to the entire community. Tressie McMillian writes that sexual abuse marks Black girls and the women they become as a sacrifice for more critical conversations on race to emerge. The sacrifice is that the abuse, which often may be enacted in the space of the home first, becomes collapsed and marked as promiscuous. McMillan writes, "For Black girls, home is both refuge and where your most intimate betrayals happen. . . . Home is where they love you until you're a ho."[24] "What About" is impactful because it is a first-person narrative delivered by an entertainer talking about their abuse in a direct way. There is no ambiguity in that song, just power in affirming others to name the abuse that you're experiencing.

The co-creator, writer, and director of *Pose* (2018–), the critically acclaimed New York City–set television series focusing on queer and trans ballroom performers of color in the 1980s and 1990s, Janet Mock (who named herself Janet after the singer) discussed how the explicit raw nature of songs like "What About" transformed her life. Janet was a Black popular vocalist documenting her pain in a manner that may parallel other Black women in society.[25] Mock's own frankness about her journey to self-actualization in her memoir *Redefining Realness: My Path to Womanhood, Identity, Love & So Much More* has provided a similar impact to trans women of color. Janet herself knew that the song needed to be frank in order for her narrative to not be misinterpreted and hoped that such honesty would inspire others who saw themselves in the song to do the same. She states,

> I did another song on the *Janet* album that was called "This Time" which talked about it and I guess I just never got over that part of my life, because I felt the need to write about it again. It was kind of tough time. But I think it's important to let others know that certain things that you may have experienced in your life, and that they're not alone, and that you understand what they're going through, and that they can get through it.[26]

Janet's decision to perform "What About" for a fashion awards show was an insurgent one. She occupied a space heavily marketed to women. Janet wanted to intervene in the public to share her trauma with other women in hopes of affirming her abuse and theirs in that shared space and to the audience at home.

Janet was no stranger to rock, having successfully proved her proficiency with the chart-topping "Black Cat" (1986) and then again with *janet.*'s "This Time." "What About" mixes heavy rock with the "traditional patterns of blues discourse." Janet conveys the latter by narrating her life to "us" and not to her ex-lover. This is evident by the pronoun use of "he" as opposed to "you" when she sings the verses. The crucial shift to the declarative "you" that emerges in the chorus is Janet learning from her own story to speak up about her turmoil. The structure of the song plays out as an attempt to relive and intervene on a past memory in her life. A moment in which marriage was proposed and she may have silenced her screaming thoughts by acquiescing to the request.

The last few iterations of the chorus feature the singer telling her abuser off. She stated in her *Ebony* magazine interview that the memories of this relationship continue to haunt her and that making the decision to leave was difficult, revealing that she "got her ass kicked for it." However severe that consequence may have been, Janet informed *Ebony*'s Laura B. Randolph that she probably would not be there if she had not left, pointing to painful reality that domestic violence usually ends in death.

In "What About," Janet does not practice the classic "call and response" tactic used in the blues. A call and response would be similar to a "Hey Ladies," or "Listen up Girls," chant delivered by the singer to invite the audience to pay attention as the singer is about to share some truth. Although this is missing from the song, Janet proposes in its omission that she is speaking some truth to herself and for anyone else who might be listening in. This opens the space in the song for Janet to be both the one delivering "the truth" and a listener in the audience because she is, and will be, in need of some truth as well.

3
Damn, Disconnected

"Got 'Til It's Gone"

Janet hit the airwaves in September 1997 with a more mature voice. Melancholy lyrics made *The Velvet Rope*'s first single, "Got 'Til It's Gone," a sorrowful pastiche, a masterpiece as some critics noted. Many reviewers noted, however, that despite the song's "wise" lyrics, its hip-hop-driven focus would be a "hard" sell on pop radio. Jam acknowledged the difficulty in pushing the song through to a larger audience and noted the difference in reception between "I Get Lonely" and "Got 'Til It's Gone," which carry some sonic and lyrical similarities but received different receptions from mainstream pop radio.[1] Part of the difference may have been the public's unfamiliarity with Janet's new, experimental sound. Janet's turn to hip-hop for *The Velvet Rope* is similar to her citation of early blues music in that it was a turn to using music styles historically rooted in Black cultural production. Hip-hop emerges in the Bronx, New York, in the 1970s as an aesthetic that centered audience engagement through sampling, orality (a smooth-spoken flow over a beat), DJ'ing, and rapping.

Hip-hop culture is the foremother for our contemporary relationship with remix culture. It is a movement of aesthetic practices delivering power to the people not only to create music but also to learn about culture through the process. During the MTV special for the *Janet World Tour* (1993–5), Janet argues that rap is a form of education: "I credit rap for teaching our kids a lot about themselves. Where they've come from . . . I know I wasn't taught that in school. I've only ever known of us as being slaves and that was it, not kings and queens."[2] Rap reminds its audience of Black histories absent from dominant institutions. It is a genre that works to disalienate Black and Brown individuals in society, and that helped disalienate Janet by educating her about her cultural history.

In *Black Skin, White Masks*, Frantz Fanon argued for the disalienation of Black humanity. He writes, "We shall see that the alienation of the Black man is not an individual question but a social one."[3] What Fanon's argument reveals is how Black individuals may experience a form of alienation that is racialized, meaning that the isolation they feel is marked and caused by the racialization of their body in predominantly white spaces. The alienation of the Black body is a learned process emerging in the educational system. In her 1997 *Newsweek* interview, Janet detailed a particularly hurtful experience in which a white woman educator chastised her for not knowing the answer to a question, which led the class to mock Janet's inactivity. She followed that anecdote by stating, "Some of my teachers weren't nice to me. I remember when I got my first Black teacher. I was in fourth grade. Mrs. Cheryl Womack. And I thought she was the most beautiful thing. And she was such a sweet lady and so kind to me. Not all my Caucasian teachers were mean, but I had a couple that weren't nice to me at all."[4] For a brief year, Janet felt less alone because her educational needs were addressed by someone who was less likely to cause harm to her psyche based on her race and gender. While not lyrically stated in the album, some of the isolation discussed in *The Velvet Rope* was forged from experiences of racialized alienation in predominantly white spaces, from her classroom to the music industry.

When you hear the DJ scratch at the beginning of "Got 'Til It's Gone," Janet and company were situating themselves in a community racialized as Black and Brown. The centering of that community may have dissuaded mainstream radio stations to share what she had to say. Hip-hop's community carries a very specific racial praxis to its production and performance that can educate others outside of a Black and Brown community about a way of living, a history different to theirs. Janet signaled that possibility of a cross-cultural dialogue exchange in the song by sampling Joni Mitchell.

"Joni Mitchell never lies." Released as the first single for the album on September 22, 1997, "Got 'Til It's Gone" cited the wisdom of Joni Mitchell's "Big Yellow Taxi"—Mitchell's 1971 single that narrates the ecological transformations occurring due to capitalist production and exploitation of natural resources. Over the chorus she warns the listeners, "Don't it always seem to go/ That you don't know what you've got 'til it's gone"—wisdom that went unheeded. Despite the sample of Joni Mitchell's breathless voice, "Got 'Til It's Gone" was a harsher song than Janet's previous singles and was certainly more depressing. In the mid-tempo song, Janet mourns the loss of a lover, long gone, and challenges time itself as a remedy. Janet does not end the song with a resolution of reconciliation; time turns her feelings into—like all things—dust.

Loss of love in women's cultural production is a classic trope: the grieving widow, the scorned woman, and the jilted lover. How do women participate in the cultural production of loss, knowing that the work will be used against us? Despite the need to produce music that demonstrates women's cultural production outside of relationships, women know that they will have to grapple with that dichotomy in order to affirm their life experiences in their art. And, at times, that includes producing work from and about emotional loss (musician Björk spoke about this difficulty when making her album about love loss, 2015's *Vulnicura*).[5] What did Q-Tip and Janet say again? *Joni Mitchell never lies.*

Joni Mitchell's career is unique not just for being a woman singer-songwriter in a genre largely dominated by men in the 1970s, but also for her insistence on creative control over the production of her work. A feat that was hard fought and won by Mitchell in the early 1970s. Mitchell's second self-produced studio album (fourth album overall), *Blue* (1971), has been lauded for its emotional rawness and bravado in documenting her emotional turmoil, glee, and recovery from two relationships. The frank discussion of her feelings in *Blue* has been an influence on many singer-songwriters, so it makes sense that her work would shape Janet's as well. *The Velvet Rope* bears many similarities with

Mitchell's *Blue*. These two albums mark women at a turning point in their emotional and creative journeys and provide templates for other women to follow. In this way, the Mitchell citation could be considered essential for Janet's journey in exploring and accepting loss as a woman.

Reviewers, though, were dumbfounded and in awe by the citation of Mitchell in Janet's "urban" song.[6] Of all the samples on the album, Janet had to defend her citation of "Big Yellow Taxi" the most. Janet repeatedly had to proclaim admiration of Mitchell and to mention how her brother Randy introduced her to Mitchell's work. And as it turns out, the admiration was mutual. Mitchell invited Janet to participate in the cover album, *A Tribute to Joni Mitchell* (2007), which underwent many years of production and ultimately left Janet's contribution ("The Beat of Black Wings") out of the final mix.[7] Another expression of admiration by Mitchell emerged during an intimate 1998 performance for fans where Mitchell incorporated Q-Tip's ending refrain from "Got 'Til It's Gone."[8] The reason why Mitchell was a "surprise" citation for Janet to many critics/reviewers speaks more of the limited citations they think were possible for Janet to engage with. In the years since the release of "Got 'Til It's Gone," many reviewers have now favorably compared *The Velvet Rope* to Mitchell's *Blue* for the emotional and sonic risks taken, including her collaboration with Mitchell and Q-Tip.

Mitchell and Q-Tip's inclusion created a fusion of rock, pop, rap, and soul.[9] Q-Tip's smooth flow lessens the blow of his negative response to his ex-lover's pleas of remorse and reconciliation. Prior to and just after Q-Tip's rap, his voice can be heard conversing statements and declarations throughout the song. These interjections produce a laid-back demeanor that matches the groove. Who talks during a song? This informal dynamic is heightened by Janet's laughter toward the end, which rapturously gives the song some much-needed levity. Additionally, Janet opens "Got 'Til It's Gone" by asking what the next song is. The question allows for Q-Tip to respond but also allows a momentary rupture of the narrative arc. Why is she asking *us* what the next song is, it's *her* album, shouldn't *she* know? The casual demeanor serves to bring the artist and the production "down to our level," she is a part of this listening experience as well.

"Empty"

For some of us, the "Interlude: Online" opens with a hauntingly familiar sound of a dial-up modem. In the early days of the internet that dial would sonically signal our connection to the virtual, "judgement-free," world of the web—a world that many of us now seek to frequently disconnect from due to its toxicity. Sonic familiarity can trigger vivid memories in ways the visual is unable to. I still recall the painfully slow process of watching the yellow AOL avatar running to connect me to the World Wide Web whenever I hear a dial-up modem. "Online" sets up the cyber chat session that "Empty" engages with through the sound of the dial-up modem followed by fingers tapping away at a thick keyboard. With the advancements of digital technology, these sounds are becoming less familiar to us and the generations that follow.

Memory and anticipation are the key players of "Empty." Lyrically, Janet is lured to her keyboard by memories of previous virtual interactions with a digital lover. In the background, we hear a series of electronic beats that push the song's technological agenda. Jam has declared "Empty," the song that he is most proud of due to its engagement with internet culture and "being ahead of its time in predicting how the internet would impact our lives."[10]

The song deals with some of the naughtier elements of online interaction. The thrills and lows of cybersex via chatrooms. The transformation of a "pure" virtual world that could be transcended through a digital screen was still a few years away from a mass market. So, Janet and her lover communicate through "textured words" instead. Janet's anticipation is heightened by her unseen, unmet chatter who simultaneously knows her pain and is able to build her fantasies through their prose. The connection with the chatter is so strong that it is able to manifest a physical response for the singer, leaving Janet licking her lips and tasting her chatter's smile through text-based conversations alone.

Since the explosion of Web 2.0.—which defines the era of user-generated online content and its social engagement—social media shapes how we see ourselves and how we interact with others. It never satisfies. Social media is driven by anticipation. A future pretense that *will* satisfy some felt desire. For example, a post *will* produce an engagement with an audience that *will* satisfy your followers and, by extension, yourself. Sometimes it does. But the fact remains, that *all social media engagement is predicated upon its future satisfactory potential.* John Berger's argument on publicity under capitalist production provides a synthesis of how internet culture, identity formation, and a feeling of political powerlessness produces and feeds into the anticipation that drives user engagement with the virtual.

> It is this which makes it possible to understand why publicity remains credible . . . the gap between what publicity actually offers and the future it promises, corresponds with the gap between what the spectator-buyer feels himself to be and what he would like to be. The two gaps become one; and instead of the single gap being bridged by action or lived experience, it is filled with glamourous day-dream.[11]

We can take Berger's commentary to be reflective of the way in which internet culture often stands in for the real or creates an anticipation for the real that is never achieved. The pursuit of the dreams it will fulfill occupies our *real* time.

Ultimately, "Empty" narrates the ennui that Janet experiences when her chatter does not respond and in her inability to determine the sincerity of her communicative friend. Janet sings about her eagerness to go home and turn her lover on and the eventual suspense she endures waiting for them to engage with her by passing time waiting. It is engagement built around suspense; all Janet can do is lie in wait. Toward the end the song, Janet wonders if she is just wasting time with them, potentially using them as a way to escape her reality. As time passes, the emotional void that Janet feels continues to grow, until she is abruptly cut off. *"Damn, disconnected."* The song immediately transitions to the "Interlude: Full" where she admonishes herself for using another person to fill herself up. Despite her effort, Janet, like so many today, is unable to escape her reality.

Taking Time

Agency, or control, has long been situated outside the realm of what is made available to Black women's lives. Not having time, or having what little time you do misused by others positions your body, your personhood in service to someone else. Your "time" is not yours but something received through others. Janet's career has long positioned her on a road for control, but with *The Velvet Rope* we hear an individual work through a possibility of self-emancipation, time for herself, knowing that women who often do are punished and deemed selfish. Legislative structures have aided in this perception in that, historically, Black women's mobility has been limited. The lack of mobility, freedom to wander even, contributed to the belief that Black women were less than deserving in taking time off for themselves.[12]

Media representation has further solidified this perception. The "unstoppable" or "strong Black woman" stereotype has propelled our social imagination on Black women not needing time, not needing space, and being unbreakable to the ills produced by societal and personal relationships. These stereotypes are particularly harmful insofar as they frame seeking help as a personal and social failure. When Audre Lorde wrote about self-care being a form of warfare for Black women, it was to draw attention to the ways in which Black women are devalued by the institution and that the lack of attentiveness to our bodies, our time, affects our health. (Lorde herself was struggling with funding treatments for her breast cancer at the time of that declaration.) To enact self-care is to be attentive to yourself and its needs in ways in which institutions, families, and society often do not provide for Black women.[13]

Janet frequently remarked that this album took so much time. *The Velvet Rope* took twice as long to record as did her previous albums, six months compared to the two to three months.[14] Jam affirms this meandering pace, her usual (over) work ethic fell apart for that project. He further stated in a twentieth anniversary interview that they would often just jam in the studio and be really "unproductive." On days when Janet would call out of a studio appearance Jam and Lewis would just work on other tracks. He stated that he did not think too much about the slower pace that the album was taking. This was the tempo of *The Velvet Rope*. The album and Janet were going to take as much time as they needed.

"Every Time"

On November 17, 1998, "Every Time" would be the sixth and final single released for the album. The B-side "Accept Me," along with disco mix of "Every Time," was also made available on the CD. "Accept Me" is a fairly straightforward ballad in which Janet asks an unnamed addressee for acceptance of who she is. Given that she was married at the time, songs like "Accept Me" and "Every Time" point to a schism in her romantic relationship. Due to an agreement achieved as part of the divorce settlement in 2000, Janet is legally prohibited from publicly commenting on her time with Renée Elizondo Jr.[15] Thus, there is little information Janet has publicly provided with regard to what was happening with her love life during the time of the album's production. Elizondo Jr. claims co-writing credit on the album and was *very* vocal during *The Velvet Rope* promotion about his participation in all of Janet's success from the *Rhythm Nation 1814* era to the present, an odd yet discerning detail. In *True You*, Janet admits that part of the experiences that led to *The Velvet Rope* was the breakdown of emotional intimacy she was experiencing. She states, "The relationship I was in that had brought comfort now showed signs of serious strains."[16]

"Every Time" features an emotionally vulnerable Janet discussing how each of her relationships seems to fall apart. In interviews she remarked that she would not have been able to pursue these thoughts without being in a stable relationship and I believe her.[17] I think part of the sadness that emerges from *The Velvet Rope* is the artist's reconciling with falling out of love with someone who may still be committed to you, even if it is just your career. "Every Time" finds the singer wondering if she would be able to find the strength to put herself out there again. The process of being emotionally available to another person is labor intensive. It is a process made more complicated for Black women. Society, and by extension our interpersonal relationships that replicate societal power imbalances of race and gender, demands more labor and time from Black women in order for them to exist.

The video for "Every Time" was directed by fine art photographer/artist Matthew Rolston. Unlike the other videos for *The Velvet Rope*, "Every Time" features Janet's hair back to black. Janet's tresses are much looser than the corkscrew curls that dominated the promotional tour. Her hair now reaches past her shoulders. She wears green contacts and nothing else. She sings to the camera in aqua-driven environments at the Therme Vals spa in Vals, Graubünden, in the Swiss Alps. The video features high-speed underwater shots of dancers wearing flowing, chiffon-like aqua and green garments with shots of Janet nearly submerged underwater. This effect was achieved by using the then latest technological changes to camera to capture a lot of movement quickly. The nearly submerged Janet scenes create a visual metaphor of her baring her emotional vulnerability through the cleansing properties of water.

The video is purely meant to provide visual pleasure to the audience in that it arrests our senses through design, aesthetics, and bodies. This is a *feeling* video and in drawing out the pleasure of feeling, which does not always suggest erotic, the video is able to amplify Janet's emotional state of mind. Though "Every Time" may not have been a "success" at the time of its release, it definitely influenced a generation of pop stars to visually amplify the vulnerability in their ballads by becoming emotionally vulnerable through water, most notably evident in Britney Spears's "Everytime" and Rihanna's "Stay." The last shot of the video features one of the underwater performers removing their chiffon garment for the camera to zoom in to a tattoo of the Sankofa symbol covering their back. In her final single and video from *The Velvet Rope*, Janet alerts her audience that the feeling of neglect and abandonment was coming back again. The key difference is Janet's ability to learn how to process pain as opposed to burying those emotions within her.

"God's Stepchild"

For the Japanese release of the album, Janet included a bonus track. "God's Stepchild" was wedged between "Special" and the hidden track "Can't Be Stopped." The song is quite melodic and carries a similar piano-driven compositional quality to her 1993 single, "Again." Janet becomes introspective about her loneliness and isolation. Even the title alone is evocative: if we are "all God's children," who could inhabit the role of being "their" stepchild? "Never felt pretty/Learned to just pretend," Janet sings again emphasizing her life-long habit of escapism or being for others in the world. Lyrically, Janet belabors the existential and physical plight of not being enough for anyone. Further along, she admonishes her habit of keeping depressive thoughts to herself out of a desire to not burden anyone with her woes.

The last verse of the song finds Janet recognizing the need to have that voice of encouragement come from within. Janet would clarify this sentiment in *True You*, where she affirms that her parents, while loving and caring, did not have the psychological insight to help her through her crises and her feelings of inadequacy.[18] She devotes a chapter, "As Pretty As" to examine her feelings of inferiority to her eldest sister,

Rebbie. Very few people were available (or trained) to help her combat body dysmorphia at a young age when Janet convinced herself that she had the wrong shape. "How do you start feeling good about yourself when feeling bad has been a life-long pattern?"[19] If the song suggests that the voice of affirmation needs to come from within then it hinges upon a sad truth that many individuals in this world may only have themselves to rely on as a source for love and affirmation.

"I Get Lonely"

Of all the despair that is heard in *The Velvet Rope*, "I Get Lonely" is the synthesis of the album's mood. Sometimes loneliness cannot be solved with the presence of another body. In "I Get Lonely," Janet fully embraces loss. To be vulnerable is to put yourself at risk, and all relationships demand that risk. "I Get Lonely" captures that contradiction, the need to feel for others, to be vulnerable, and the desire to protect oneself at the expense of being vulnerable. To paraphrase a key line from the film *Mahogany* (1975), "It's hard to feel for someone when you can barely keep yourself up."

"I Get Lonely" both invites comfort and simultaneously rebukes it. Janet is pleading for sympathy, to be held and cared for, but she will not accept that care from just anyone. "Can't let/ Just anybody hold me." Janet expresses how familiar living in a state of misery can be. The real risk in "I Get Lonely" is learning to build an identity beyond the one forged through injury. Janet is at a precipice, seeking the love of another and recognizing that relationship's impending doom and ultimately being alone again with her fears. How do you leave your demons behind when your demons are the only friends you've had?

I routinely joke with my friends that my depression is my best friend. That's a lie. I say that joke to myself. While my depression may not actually be my best friend, it is my longest relationship. Although I manage my depression to the best of my ability, I do fear waking up one morning to find it *not there*. I, like so many others, struggle with the prospect of possessing an identity that is not rooted in injury when injury is the only framework I have been able to see myself through. I write this neither to seek advice nor to give advice but merely to acknowledge that to be vulnerable as a "wounded" woman can be a painful state to be in—I know this firsthand. "I Get Lonely" is the struggle to move away from sites of injury and pursue vulnerability at all costs. It is a song that has occupied the majority of my listening engagements with the album as I continue to find a state of being not located in pain.

"I Get Lonely" was the third song released for the album and would prove to be the right song to carry over the smash success of the album's second single, "Together Again." Jam stated that the song seemed to capture and marry the pop success of "Together Again" with the "urban" vibe that failed to connect listeners of "Got 'Til It's Gone." "I Get Lonely" was receiving heavy airplay on urban and pop stations.[20] When looking at Janet's singles, the selection of "I Get Lonely" can be considered a "risky" one. Although no stranger to taking musical risks, Janet's previous albums all included a serious ballad that would top the charts early on. "Let's Wait Awhile" on *Control*, "Come Back to Me" on *Rhythm Nation 1814*, and "Again," from *janet.*, all of which were successful on the charts. It's not accidental that she would often perform those songs in a ballad melody during her tours.

Following the template she set out for herself, it would have made sense for Janet to follow up "Together Again" with (the eventual sixth single) "Every Time" or "Anything." Instead, she chose a song that subverted the flow of a traditional ballad. The video features heavy choreography aided by the finger snap beat appearing in the background. If Janet was on the verge of a break down, it was gonna be a smooth one. The song gained further popularity aided by the "TNT Remix" featuring Blackstreet. Much like the inclusion of Q-Tip on "Got 'Til It's Gone," Janet was making collaborative decisions that placed her in dialogue with the changing landscape of hip-hop and Black culture in the late 1990s.

The seventeen mixes for "I Get Lonely" extend the song's hip-hop structure by drawing out a variety of backing beats that are somewhat subdued in the album version. The added beats in the mix then make Janet's bridge break down more pronounced, almost mirroring a break heard in a swing jazz song. The majority of these mixes are variations of the main mix (LP version, radio edit, video edit, etc.) and the "TNT Remix" featuring Blackstreet with some versions omitting their vocals but keeping the heavier beats. The "Jam and Lewis Feel My Bass Mix" not only amps up the bass but incorporates added samples from previous Janet songs, including the "Here We Go Now" lyric from "Throb" and the "1,2,3,4" heard in "Empty." The "Extended Street Remix," which also includes backing vocals from Blackstreet, draws out the hip-hop flow of the song and even locates this harder beat and beatboxing as a product of cultural practices in the "streets" of Black communities. Many of these mixes have a radio edit, suggesting they were being marketed for urban radio airplay. This is also supported by the "listenability" of the remixes in that they retain the album version's lyrics. As an aside, it appears that many of the US copies of the single feature the pink ribbon used to raise awareness to breast cancer in the liner notes.[21]

The "TNT Remix" features loops in the help of Timberland to move the backing beats to the foreground in addition to the vocals provided by Blackstreet.[22] Lyrically, the mix is similar to the album version, with Teddy Riley taking on the second verse. "Our remix particularly has Blackstreet vocals and it's going to take a bit of time for everyone to start understanding and start adjusting to her, which she's done it many times before," Riley explained to the BBC for a making-of featurette. Eric Williams added "it's very different and she's a great artist." What Riley and Williams's remark suggests is that the "difference" that is being pushed through in her music is Janet's placing herself in dialogue with a hip-hop group. The musical feature, the guest rap, the guest lyric that dominates many pop singles today was still a nascent practice for mainstream pop artists like Janet, and the "TNT remix" (along with Mariah Carey's *Fantasy* remix with Ol' Dirty Bastard [1995]) helped pioneer that crossover appeal. The addition of Blackstreet on the "TNT remix" draws out the more seductive, sensual qualities of the song. "I Get Lonely" has a swagger to its themes of isolation with a subtle suggestion that if no one else can hold her, if no one else can satisfy her loneliness, then, just maybe, she'll have to "take care" of herself.

4
Mmm . . . My Lips Hurt

Your coochie is goin' to swell up and fall apart.
—*Uncredited female voice, "Interlude: Speaker Phone"*

"Interlude: Speaker Phone"

An interlude. And, some speculation. While I stated that I am not interested in speculating on Janet's life beyond what she has been willing to admit to, I will momentarily suspend that practice to indulge in some gossip. The interlude that precedes Janet's lustful blues track, "My Need," is "Speaker Phone." It is the most explicit track on the album and alludes to same-gender sexual dynamics. While some fans have speculated that the other woman's voice is Shawnette Heard, one of Janet's background dancers, I disagree.[1] In the interlude that precedes "Go Deep," "Fasten Your Seatbelts" Janet enlists the voices of Tina Landon, Kelly Konno, and Shawnette Heard. In interviews, Janet was quite vocal about the interpersonal relationship with her dancers in that they were all tomboys growing up and quickly bonded over that shared history. Her dancers, affectionately referred to as "the kids," were her friends, and Janet was happy to acknowledge them whenever possible.

So, if the voice on the other end was Heard, I find it suspicious that Janet would not credit her. I suspect there are two reasons the other voice on "Speaker Phone" is left uncredited. One, it leaves the relationship ambiguous, just exactly who would she call with ease to openly (and perhaps routinely) masturbate on the phone with? Secondly, it might have been to preserve the identity of the recipient's voice of this illicit call. Fans, including this author, have widely speculated that recipient to be Lisa Marie Presley, Janet's ex sister-in-law. After all, Presley was infamously Janet's date to *The Velvet Rope* listening party in September 1997, which also counted Marilyn Manson, Billy Corgan, and Naomi Campbell as attendees. Additionally, Janet thanks a "Lisa" in the liner notes for *The Velvet Rope* with the following note: "Lisa, you crazy as hell, girl. I am your belayer. I love yo crazy ass!"[2] And before you say it *could* be *any* "Lisa," Janet used a near similar vocabulary to describe her friendship with Presley when talking about her to Oprah in 1997. Given the explicit nature of "Interlude: Speaker Phone" one might ask, just what kind of relationship did Janet have with her ex sister-in-law?

"Speaker Phone" opens with a sample of the chorus "I Get Lonely" followed by a dial tone and the phone ringing; we are listening in on this conversation from Janet's perspective. A woman's voice answers the call, with Janet informing the woman that it's "her." The intimacy of the conversation is established in the lack of names and the informality of the address. "You got me on that damn, speaker phone again," the woman says, making it clear that Janet has done this before. When asked what the singer could possibly be doing with her hands that would necessitate the use of a speaker phone, Janet giggles and tells her not to worry about as she is taking care of her business. Janet invites the unnamed woman out for the night, only for her speech to be interrupted by a soft moan. The interlude concludes with the woman telling Janet that her "coochie is going to swell up and fall apart."

"Speaker Phone" stuns. The queer intimacy of casually masturbating on the phone to a friend while inviting them out to party speaks volumes to the way in which women's same-gender friendship may include frank discussions and opportunities to bond over and through sexual encounters. Moreover, Janet's interlude further solidifies that space for queer bonding with the inclusion of "I Get Lonely." In opening "Speaker Phone" with "I Get Lonely" and to have that same interlude precede "My Need" might be Janet's way of telling her lover that if he cannot connect with her, she will find that satisfaction (sexually and emotionally) from herself and from the women in her life. In this way, "Speaker Phone" opens the audience's ears and imaginations to Janet's fluid sexuality but also to the very real possibility of women's sexual satisfaction that they have historically provided to one another.

Sistagirls in the Life

As stated in "Like the Blues Need the Pain," race often overdetermines the visibility and analysis of Black women's lives, leaving little room to make sense of how race intersects with their gender identity. More importantly, the overdetermination of race in examining and narrating Black women's lives conceals many opportunities to make sense of their sexuality, creating false determinations that Black life predominately exists heterosexual couplings.

During the period of Reconstruction in the United States, discourse on Black women's sexuality was tied to its reproductive potential. As Slavery stripped the possibility for autonomous familial reproduction among Black individuals, Black sexual politics during Reconstruction strongly centered and advocated for the reproduction of the Black family. Sexual behaviors outside of the aims of securing the Black family's structure were seen as—what Rhonda Williams classifies as—a "betrayal to authentic Blackness."[3] Furthermore, forms of sexuality that contributed to "black excess" (the same excess that Motown's Maxine Powell urged Black women performers to not convey through their image), be that queer or "hyper" sexual performances by Black women, were viewed as an alliance to white supremacy. The representation of Black sexual politics and the demand for respectability centered Black women's performances as models to follow and ultimately condemn when not in line with Black familial structures. The surest condemnation to affect Black women is to suggest that their bodily behavior is a betrayal to the race.[4]

Black critical scholarship and art on sexuality, let alone Black women's sexuality, have remained resistant to open engagement with "creative relationships"—specifically, Black women's creative engagement with other women. Creative relationships cultivate an openness for Black women to explore sexuality outside of the dominant heterosexual framing. In so doing, these relationships posit a chance for Black women to not "accept powerlessness, or those supplied states of being that are not native" to oneself.[5] Therefore, positioning sexuality as an integral part of Black women's subject hood acknowledges the erased and silent history of our sexualities. There still remains an urgency for Black women to continue to write critically from their bodies and desires as it still, *yes still*, serves as a counterargument to contemporary colonial discourse that limits the representation of Black women's sexualities.

When my mother caught me kissing another girl in my room at the age of eleven, she called my aunt and my sister to help her deal with me. The "devil" had gotten ahold of me. In our living room, I was forced to affirm a sexuality that was not mine as my aunt, mother, and sister gazed down and asked whether I was gay. I knew that me kissing girls did not negate my attraction for the opposite gender but I was informed in that space that attraction existed solely to one gender or the other. I informed my family that I must be gay. That was that. My mother's upbringing was largely influenced by the same modes of respectability that shaped Katherine and Janet's upbringing. The burden we place on poor Black women to be representative of the race comes at great costs that often see Black women never pursuing their desires and limiting what types of women they could be and would want to be in the world.

My mother cried, yelled at, and sent me to my room after that forced confession. I was grounded for being sexually confused (or gay, in her eyes). I remember crying in bed, afterward, cradling my discman and listening to my mother's copy of *The Velvet Rope*, which I managed to steal without her knowledge sometime when I was nine. "Free Xone" marked another first for me in its affirmation of bisexuality. Maybe it's the way I remember it, maybe it was always that way, but in that moment the last verse of the song where Janet narrates an encounter of a girl losing her boyfriend only to get her girlfriend back leapt out to me as if it was hidden in all my past listens. I felt heard in that song but I did not have a name for what I was hearing or feeling, just a space in a song.

"Free Xone"

"Free Xone" is Janet at her most experimental and her funkiest. The song is similar to the sonic thrill and house music throb on *janet*. The song opens with Janet informing us that her nickname used to be "Mama Yoke." In a fan-compiled dataset of celebrity pseudonyms, Mama Yoke was Janet's nickname in/at lesbian clubs/circles. The song features Janet narrating an airplane encounter with a displeased male passenger upon finding out their seatmate is gay—"Let's get Free!" is proclaimed by a crowd of voices on the track. The title of the track refers to both the free structure and the sonic zone in the song free from bigotry, namely homophobia. The use of the x as opposed to the z for zone is suggestive of the structural experimentation as well as the connections to sexuality. The song is not x-rated but exists in that other space that cannot always be named *this* or *that*.

The song samples three different classic funk songs. The most immediate and recognizable sample is Archie Bell & the Drells' 1968 song "Tighten Up," with many commentators suggesting that it is one of the earliest funk songs to hit the airwaves. "Tighten Up" is funk jam about mellowing out to the beat during times of strife (this song came out during the Vietnam War in which Bell was ultimately drafted to fight in). "Tighten Up" talks the listener through the process of creating "the one groove," an intense sonic flow that produces a positive force through bass lines and guitar riffs that, ultimately, distinguishes it from other Black music aesthetics. "Free Xone" takes Bell's declaration of "Now make it mellow!" and applies that need to homophobia. Essentially, Janet wants everyone to calm the fuck down with their bigotry.

Lyn Collins's "Think (About it)" from 1972 is further used throughout the song's structure, mimicking the bravado of Collins's declarative gospel style. Janet had already sampled "Think (About it)" for her 1989 single, "Alright." "Think (About it)" sits at the apex of Black musical fusion in the early 1970s and is structured around the "call and response." It is a powerful retribution to the fellas who break women's hearts and has become a key sample for R&B and hip-hop songs since its release. The last and most obscure sample is by Portland, Oregon, band Pleasure. The 1977 song "Joyous" is an R&B, jazz, and funk jam that ruminate on the finer, more luscious experiences that life has to offer. Pedagogically speaking, "Free Xone" utilizes its samples to place it in a larger genealogy of funk but also to track the progressiveness of Funk's ideology and practices. L. H. Stallings's book

Funk the Erotic points the myriad of ways that funk music has historically intersected with the erotics through its tension of performance, labor, sensory experience, aesthetics, and embodiment.

Funk demands the body to work to the beat, to sweat it out. In the performances of a funk legend like Betty Davis that work drew out the erotic potential of the genre, the performances, and the knowledge production it carried with them.[6] Funk demands that you earn that groove. Its ethos brought a visible contrast to the respectability politics of the previous Motown era and centered the body just being free. Freedom in funk was a political freedom from persecution that relied upon the history of Black cultural production to produce its practice. Freedom was in the rhythm; it was in how you danced and funked out. "Free Xone" cites that history and carries its message to the present in order to affirm and practice fluid sexuality and gender expression.

Although "Free Xone" is specific to sexuality we can take its open-ended potential to draw out larger questions of gender identity as well. Scholar Vivian Namaste's interviews point to the representational lack that gender nonconforming and trans individuals have in the media due to mainstream LGBTQ2IA+ (Lesbian, Gay, Bisexual, Transgender/sexual, Queer, Two-Spirit, Intersex, Asexual, and more) representation primarily centering (white) cis gay men as a way to "fulfill" the representation of the group as a whole. The continual collapsing of this group suggests that all parties share the same "queer" sexual orientation, this is simply not true.[7]

My purpose in addressing fluid gender identification within "Free Xone" is to be attentive to how many trans and gender-nonconforming individuals have opened the already fluid space on the song and the album to affirm their experiences in the world. Janet Mock stated in *Redefining Realness* that she found great comfort in the album listening to Janet expressing her full self, including her anger, pain, and her fluid sexuality because it gave her a space to explore her true self.[8] The ambiguity on *The Velvet Rope* is so integral in helping listeners navigate uncertainty.

The very same metaphors that were misunderstood by cismale reviewers—Danyel Smith's 1997 *Vibe*'s interview, John Norris's unsympathetic interview for MTV,[9] or Ernest Hardy's review of the album for *Rolling Stone*[10]—were the very ones that enabled Janet's fans to create, affirm, and experiment with their lives, bodies, sexualities, and identities. Reviewers like *AllMusic*'s Stephen Thomas Erlewine stated that Janet's "attempts to broaden her sexual horizon frequently sound forced, whether it's the references to piercing or her recasting of Rod Stewart's 'Tonight's the Night' as a lesbian anthem."[11] But fan reception toppled the critical reception in how we remember *The Velvet Rope*, drastically changing perception since its release. For example, the Wikipedia entry (which underwent a radical re-edit after the twentieth anniversary of the album) would suggest that the album's engagement with sexuality and identity was "critically acclaimed" from its release. This is not the case. I want to highlight the way in which digital sites can erase and edit information as they emerge, thus affecting our perception of past events. Yes, *The Velvet Rope* is *now* regarded as a masterpiece in Janet's oeuvre, but when it was released the reception was mixed.

"Tonight's the Night"

Janet used the practice of covering a song to align her body with the original song's message and to expand its meaning. In her famous 1993 *Rolling Stone* interview, "The Joy of Sex," Janet explained and defended her cover of Johnny Daye's 1968 song "What'll I Do for Satisfaction." Janet discussed at length her evolving relationship to sex over the years suggesting that, for her, this change needed to be in line with her consciousness. She stated, "Sex has been an important part of me for several years. But it just hasn't blossomed publicly until now. I've had to shed some old attitudes before feeling completely comfortable with my body. Listening to my new record, people intuitively understand the change in me." In this response, Janet makes two things clear: first, that her continual sexual emergence was not only ongoing but one that is a direct response to her childhood; and second, she alerts the reader that the creative expression on the record is largely defined by her hand in that she began to take more authorship over not just the lyrics but the composition, production, and beat making for each of the songs on *janet.*

In her 1993 cover of Johnny Daye's "What'll I Do," Janet emphasizes her demand for satisfaction by sampling the Rolling Stone's "(I can't get no) Satisfaction" from 1965. The trajectory of this cover led her to work with Dave Navarro (who was then a member of the Red Hot Chili Peppers) on

MMM . . . MY LIPS HURT

the remix of the song in 1995. I am fascinated by Janet's desire to subvert the power and identity of classic rock songs about sex to introduce and make clear a Black woman's demand for satisfaction. Her experience with "What'll I Do" help shape her approach to covering Rod Stewart's 1976 "Tonight's the Night (Gonna Be Alright)." Janet's cover (and her history of covers) performs a surrogation. Surrogation defines the ways performers will use their bodies to "evoke an absence, to body something forth, especially something from a distant past," in an effort to generate alternatives around that absence or to potentially fill that absence through the performance. Rock performances (and songs) often "ritualistically traffic in performances that carry the memory of forgotten substitutions that did materialize."[12]

Janet surrogates the male singer wooing his potential "conquest," maintaining the female gender pronouns of the seducee throughout in "Tonight's the Night." The vocality of Jackson's performance is a far cry from the hard and mellow edges she exudes throughout the album. It is Janet in classic rock crooner mode. In Jackson's surrogation, she provides listeners with an image and voice of a Black pop and R&B singer embodying the ritual performance of authority and control usually inhabited by white men in rock. She insists on maintaining the gender pronouns until the last iteration of the chorus where she switches it up, "just for fun." She also lays claim to women's bodies and their satisfaction that she will deliver upon in the same way men so often do but rarely achieve (if statistics around heterosexual women's orgasms are to be believed.).

The affirmation for same-gender relationships heard on "Free Xone" and "Tonight's the Night" would lead for several interviewers to ask Janet if she was gay. She denied this claim in some interviews but her response to an MTV journalist was more ambiguous, "A lot of people have been asking am I gay. So, what is she? She likes girls or what? And the thing is, what does it matter?"[13] I am equally interested in both Janet's allyship to the LGBTQ2IA+ community performed in the songs "Free Xone" and "Tonight's the Night" and the "risky" suggestion of her own attraction to women/bisexuality. After all, she began "Free Xone" by reminding us that her name used to be "Mama Yoke." What the context is and who called her that we may never know but the ambiguity remains. The ambiguity leaves that question open and much like the songs, free.

Excess Flesh

While Janet was criticized for her risqué sexual frankness on *The Velvet Rope* and later on *All For You*, she would pay a huge toll for her lyrics on *Damita Jo*, which were used in dialogue with her 2004 Super Bowl half-time performance. We all know the performance. When discussing the structure of this book with a colleague, she informed me how bizarre it was that the image of Janet's exposed breast was imprinted in their memory despite not watching the performance nor their interest in actively pursuing the image on their own. We've all seen it. The image was dispersed widely across news programs in the following months after the performance.

What did this media coverage of a non-intentional breast exposure accomplish? The media's interest in dissecting the incident ad nauseam was aided by detailed readings of lyrics from *Damita Jo* to "prove" that Janet was "perverse" and may have had a sinister desire to "expose" herself to "wholesome" families across the nation on live TV.

The backlash was severe. Les Moonves, then head chairman and CEO of CBS Television, blackballed Janet's career and the promotion of *Damita Jo*. This information has recently become public during the investigation of Moonves over numerous allegations of inappropriate sexual conduct and harassment. And, this study has nothing to say of the fact that Justin Timberlake's career was not only not targeted but was immediately welcomed back into the industry after his tearful acknowledgment of the difficulty *he* endured while accepting a Grammy Award in 2004—a response that was met with thunderous applause. Janet's invitation to the award ceremony was revoked.[14] The eventual silencing of Janet's image was a way for patriarchal systems and for the men that uphold and benefit from them to punish her for the sexual autonomy she exhibited outside of that performance. As Shayne Lee writes,

> Obscenity is socially defined, and obscenity laws support patriarchal power relations within society. Although it might be somewhat disheartening that Janet later apologizes instead of protecting her right to expose herself in the same manner that men do, her Super Bowl surprise is nevertheless a treasonable act in society that, as Susan Bordo points out, tacitly and legally demands women to discipline their breasts.[15]

The body has long been an extension for Black women's sexuality. Nicole Fleetwood defines the frequent use of Black female artists' use of their body as a strategic enhancement of excess flesh. Excess flesh, as a strategy, signposts historical attempts to regulate Black women's bodies and to "challenge debates . . . about what constitutes positive or productive representation of Blackness by refusing the binary of negative and positive" images.[16] The flesh, like the skin, is an attribute of the body that has historically and theoretically been used to demarcate the spaces of "otherness." In the backlash to Janet after the Super Bowl performance, we can see the disciplining measures and discourse used to represent her body, and by extension her sexuality, as detrimental to social values. Janet came to represent for a larger audience what happens when you take sex "too far." It hurts you, the nation, and the race of your people. It is a testament to Janet's sense of emancipation that she continued to maintain and proudly assert her sexual autonomy in the years that followed that performance.

"Rope Burn"

Janet had to routinely clarify her interest in bondage discipline, submission, sadomasochism (BDSM) and to underscore that she was into "soft rope burn" and light, sensual pain that gives way to pleasure. The photos that accompanied the album suggest anything but "softness" though. In one of the more infamous portraits shot by von Unwerth, we see Janet in a blue latex catsuit with a hoop ring pierced through the fabric to make her nipple piercing visible. One hand is crouched upon her red mane of curls and the other hand features a stainless steel ice pick attached to a finger glove that she uses to prick her derrière. Janet's facial expression is one that makes an *oohh* to her photographer. This is my favorite composition of Janet; it is widely daring for what it reveals and conceals at the same time—the nipple piercing, the latex catsuit, the interest in pain, the confidence, and the way the whole image exudes sexuality without showing us the flesh. I am drawn to this image for the way it foreshadows Janet's eventual progression and visible exhibition of harder BDSM culture as expressed in further images and stage performances following *The Velvet Rope*. It is an image, like the song, that educates an audience on sexual consent and thus removes the stigma of advocating for alternative sexual practices.

For some, Janet's honesty about role play and submission was not to be believed. It was just a contrived way to sell records. One journalist wrote that Janet is more believable singing about heartache than she is talking about the whips and stuff on "Rope Burn."[17] "Rope Burn" is a crucial song about sex because it uncovers that it is not enough for Black women to speak out about good sex but to also assert authority over what satisfies them and the conditions that produce good sex, asking for what you want sexually. The dismissal of "Rope Burn" is emblematic of the ways in which society labels women's sexual requests as demanding or excessive. The pushback to "Rope Burn" reveals the discomfort we collectively inherited from a patriarchal society around sexual consent. The lyrics to "Rope Burn" feature consent at every corner with Janet asking her lover what they like, what she wants, and if they feel comfortable participating in that exchange.

"Rope Burn" ends with a series of shivering gasps and moans. Not only do the tone and mood of the song enable audiences to imagine Janet receiving pleasure but they tap into our senses as to *how* and *what* "good" love *sounds* and *feels* like. Speech is not the only form of communication within the song. "When women clarify the terms for sexual desires through tone, pitch, and mood" they point to why simply not stating the conditions for sexual satisfaction, autonomy, and freedom is not enough.[18] The body carries its own communicative practices, and Janet replicates those practices on the song to embody that engagement for herself and for others. She asks her lover to make her moan loudly to be sure that they can understand and respond to her desires. The moans in "Rope Burn," and elsewhere on the album, produce an affective technology, as Stallings argues, that sustains interpersonal engagements in hopes of improving the lives and sexual encounters of Black women, their partners, and anyone else who may be listening in.[19]

The song normalizes consent and creative agency over how a woman receives satisfaction. Janet might be playing a "submissive" role, but she is dedicated and equally participating in the pleasure received from that position. The song, as Janet declared, is BDSM-lite, but its declaration of BDSM introduces listeners to the basic principle of BDSM: consent. For many women, growing up in a patriarchal society means that their introduction to BDSM may also be their first encounter with communicating consent with a partner and having their sexual demands affirmed and taken seriously. Returning to her 1993 "Joy of Sex" interview, Janet spent time expressing the importance of communication around sex. She states that as a woman who finally feels good enough about her sexuality,

> . . . to demand a man's respect. It's insulting to be seen as some object; he must call her by name. It's not a brazen demand—I didn't want to be obnoxious—but I wanted to be clear. Women want satisfaction. And so do men. But to get it, you must ask for it. Know what you need. Say what you want. Sexual communication is the name of the game. Intimacy.[20]

"Anything"

Despite being written off as a copy of her 1993 love ballad "Again," "Anything" is actually a trip-hop ballad that continues "Rope Burn"'s communicative consent with a dose of emotional intimacy. On a personal note, I find "Anything" to be one of the more touching songs on the album about radical vulnerability with a lover. The inclusion of "Anything" is a testament to Janet's declaration for not just sexual autonomy but a desire to maintain intimacy with others, to keep herself emotionally available in spite of one's insecurities. When we examine the backdrop of trauma and abuse that she reveals on tracks like "What About," "You," or "My Need," the most transgressive act in the face of abuse and neglect is to remain vulnerable and to not close that capacity to care for others.

The lyrics reveal a possibility where nothing is off the table for a lover, creating more of an emotional intoxication than a purely physical one. Janet asks her lover to hold, feel, kiss, taste, and ask her for anything they may want. She follows up on her inquiries by ensuring that she will make good on her end if her lover meets her halfway, "When you do convince me/ You know that good things don't come easy." The lyrics of the song visualize an emotional and sexual see-saw with a lover. It centers pleasure but also underscores the labor or work needed to exist in a sexually and emotionally fulfilling relationship. Janet's laugh near the end of the song alleviates the flow and keeps the encounter playful. "Anything" means serious business, but it also wants that business to be "pleasurable."

The hyper-sexualization of Black popular vocalists at a young age produces a dominant representation that suggests that Black girls/women have "figured" out sex by teenage years or in their early twenties. Young Black popular vocalists in the late 1990s like Aaliyah, Beyoncé, Brandy, Monica, and others sang about "women's" problems. They sang about having sex, being sexually assertive, and having too many lovers to handle. Even when I reached sixteen and seventeen (the ages they were at the production of some of their sexually explicit songs), their supposed lived experiences were unrelatable to me and, I can assume, others. As a feminist scholar, I can analyze and recognize the production of sexuality that is often thrust upon Black girls and young women in the entertainment industry to produce a fantasy that sells. I can also recognize and affirm the agency of Black teenage girls' sexuality that exists and is often punished in communities and through institutions, experiences that are rarely represented.

Part of my interest in Janet pre and post *The Velvet Rope* comes from an appreciation of her road to sexual provocateur.[21] Gaining control of her career at the age of twenty also ensured that she expressed her sexuality on her terms and was not forced to purely sell sex.[22] Her "sexual" awakening at the age of twenty-seven and its continual manifestations since then, notably the queer ones emerging on *The Velvet Rope* at the age of thirty-one, are a counter-production to the image of sexuality performed by young pop stars. Janet's proud defense of her nipple piercing to Oprah will always stand out in my mind as an example of this counter-production. Not for its provocation but for the context that Janet gave about finally achieving bodily autonomy in her thirties. Janet's road to sexual discovery was one rooted in self-actualization and gave a place for young people to feel sexually confused and insecure amid a landscape that equates personal, financial, and social success with sexual value in your youth.

As a Black popular vocalist, Janet's introduction of non-matrimonial centered, non-heteronormative, and non-vanilla sex to pop culture is a counter-document to respectable representations of Black women's desire, even the one seen on her previous albums. Throughout the album, Janet remains firm in the pursuit of satisfaction and in reclaiming sex for herself beyond her depression and sexual insecurity. To be sure, songs from later albums like "Love Scene (Ooh Baby)" and "Would You Mind" from *All For You* as well as "Warmth" and "Moist" from *Damita Jo* would make

"Rope Burn" and "Tonight's the Night" blush by comparison. Janet is one of the rare examples of a Black popular vocalist normalizing consent, sexual experimentation, masturbation, cunnilingus, fellatio, and just plain ol' coitus through her songs. We need narratives produced by Black women on sex and consent on their own terms and not the terms of the market, because the sad reality is that many Black women are still silenced and shamed for their sexual expressions. Silencing women is an institutional practice that makes them doubtful of their sexual needs in order for their bodies and labor to be exploited by someone else. If Janet's discography is anything to stand by, she will work tirelessly to end that opportunity for exploitation of women's bodies through poetic "jouissance."

5
Work in Progress

"Go Deep"

Released as the album's fourth single on June 15, 1998, the club-inspired jam hears Janet working out her "issues" on a dancefloor. "Go Deep" is immediately preceded by the interlude "Fasten Your Seatbelts." In "Fasten Your Seatbelts" we hear Janet hanging out with (possibly) Tina Landon, Shawnette Heard, and Kelly Konno. The group egg on a member in their group to say the *classiest* line from the campy 1962 film, *What Ever Happened to Baby Jane?* Jane, played by the legendary Bette Davis, viciously taunts her sister's lack of mobility (Joan Crawford) by saying, "But you are Blanche, You are in that char!" The citation may suggest that these women are preparing for some mischief for their night out. Kelly then delivers another classic Bette Davis line from the masterful *All About Eve*, "Fasten your seatbelts. It's going to be a bumpy ride." The latter line emerges midway through the film when all hell is about to break loose as Eve (Anne Baxter) tries to throw

Davis's Margo Channing under the bus to advance her career at a dinner party. The Bette Davis citation positions the uproarious laughter heard from the group as a homage to a screen legend and gay icon who was known for her fierce independence and knack for having a good time. This citation can be heard as a specific call out to her fans in the LGBTQ2IA+ community. And, a good time is exactly what follows "Fasten Your Seatbelts" with "Go Deep."

The playful interaction from the interlude carries over to the song where Janet manages to move the party into the space of the studio. We hear the dancers chant, clap, snap, and sing along, particularly at the end where Janet removes her lead vocal from the final refrain of the chorus. Funk legend Betty Davis might have been one of the first artists to "break the sanctimonious space of the studio to bring the street vernacular of the party into the recording booth," in her 1969 song "Hangin Out" (recently released by Columbia Records in 2016)[1]—a model that would later be repeated, with more popularity, in Marvin Gaye's 1977 song "Got to Give It Up." Bringing the party into the studio is a way to capture all the different sounds of Black collectivity: bloc party, church gathering, house party. In those spaces we hear soul claps, call and response chants that mimic the engagement in spirituals, and the dialogue specific to the night out. "Go Deep" literally brings the vernacular of the club to the studio. The song speaks to the therapeutic potential of dancing away your woes with your friends. Throughout The Velvet Rope Tour promotion, Janet's interpersonal relationship with her dancers was highlighted, functioning as an extended family for the artist.

For *The Velvet Rope Tour* she asked them to each come up with a funky hairdo to match the different, freeing vibe of the album, which drew a media stir when they performed. When Janet performed on Oprah, she singled out Shawnette as she is a big fan of the media mogul since the 1985 film *The Color Purple*. The Oprah's first remark to Shawnette concerned her purple hair, at a time extreme hair colors on mainstream performers was sadly uncommon. While the dancers have changed throughout the years, Janet's practice of extended kinship with them has remained. The actress Jena Dewan, who danced on the *All for You Tour* from 2001 through 2002, has stated in numerous interviews how Janet "momed" the kids on the show and had a transparent environment for the crew and performers, which included gifting them vibrators.[2]

There were a total of thirty-four remixes created for "Go Deep." The dearth of remixes attributed to the song speaks of its targeted club appeal, as well as inviting emerging artists to collaborate or gain visibility through an official remix. The club appeal can be heard in the twelve mixes by the legendary dance and house duo "Little Louie" Vega and Kenny "Dope" Gonzalez known as Masters at Work. Masters at Work emerged in the late 1980s during the growing house music scene as it was moving from Chicago to New York. Their style often infuses soul, cut up beats, and inspiration from their Puerto Rican heritage into their collaborative process. A Masters at Work remix was known to get the party started.

Missy Elliot and Timberland contributed seven remixes for "Go Deep" but the Timberland/Missy mix of "Go Deep" stands out as it features a full rap verse by Missy Misdemeanor Elliot and adds a more consistent club groove than heard in the original production. Like the "TNT Remix" of "I Get Lonely," Janet was making conscious decisions to place herself in dialogue with the changing hip-hop landscape in her collaboration with Missy and Timberland, and she even looped in Teddy Riley, who contributed seven funk-flavored mixes. Janet often leveraged her position of pop iconicity to draw more support toward emerging hip-hop artists. The Missy remixes for "Go Deep" mark as the beginning of a richly collaborative relationship between Missy Elliot and Janet Jackson that continues to thrive to this day, including Janet's "Burnitup!"on 2015's *Unbreakable*.

Beyond the remixes, the video draws out the club atmosphere of the song and the interpersonal dynamics of Janet hanging with her friends. Directed by Jonathan Dayton and Valerie Faris, who would helm 2006 film *Little Miss Sunshine*, the video features actor Ty Hodges having an unexpected house party after his parents go out of town. The party "starts" when Janet Jackson arrives at his door, after he was just watching Janet's music videos in his room. Janet then mischievously brings her friends and dancers to Hodeges's home where a foam party erupts, caused by an overstuffed washing machine. Before he can respond to the foam emergency, Janet leads him to his room and begins to unbutton her top. As she reaches the button above her midriff the doorbell rings revealing the party and his sexual close-encounter with Janet to be a dream.

The video heavily relies on the usage of the Snorricam. The Snorricam shot is when a camera is attached to an actor's body as the background shifts behind them. This effect heightens the dynamic between the audience and the performer, and its use in a music video speaks to the way in which Janet was interested in pushing the visual dynamics of her work that move what we hear. The Snorricam shot draws out the embodied experience the audience has with the "cinematic" image and suggests that the screen can be transcended to engage with the performer that is the body centering and dictating the audience's POV. It invites audiences to experience the sensations of the characters while having "front row" access to their emotional and physical response throughout the clip. Janet, along with directors Jonathan Dayton and Valerie Faris, deploys this creative aesthetic to bring her body closer to her fans. If Janet wanted to bring her fans to the party on the other side of the velvet rope, "Go Deep" and its accompanying video are key examples of her creating possibilities for fan interconnectivity and intimacy.

Activism on the Dance Floor

On December 1, 2012, amid reports that she would be releasing new music, Janet dropped a video. Janet announced her ambassadorship with amfAR (the Foundation for AIDS Research), declaring her commitment to preserving research on HIV/AIDS as the crisis is not over and is particularly impacting communities of color the hardest. HIV/AIDS is, yes, a biological virus but it is one that spreads, and ultimately kills, due to social ills like structural inequality, racism, sexism, homophobia, and transphobia that make it difficult for those who test positive to seek and obtain care.

Of all individuals who have HIV/AIDS in the United States, 45 percent are Black despite Black Americans accounting for just 12 percent of the general population. In 2015, Black women accounted for 61 percent of the women diagnosed with HIV in the United States. This number dramatically increases when we focus on trans women: 56 percent of Black trans women have had positive diagnoses for HIV in their life. Those numbers continue to grow as a staggering 44 percent of all new HIV-positive diagnoses are delivered to bodies racialized as Black.[3] What these numbers demonstrate is that while globally the "crises" around HIV/AIDS might be placated, for Black individuals, specifically Black women, the crisis is not only ongoing but has dramatically worsened. How do we as artists, scholars, and activists conduct work on the forgotten?

Dance has long been utilized as an activist tool for engagement, production, and affirmation of one's societal or personal problems. The kinetic engagement of structuring possibility in the space of the dancefloor has long been theorized. In that dance, which is not an inherently natural state for the body to be in, works out movement to a beat. Working out the movement may lead to engaging with a dance partner, it may open up the dancer's corporeal relationship with space, it may open up the dancer's relationship with a song, and it may even open up the possibility of picking somebody up. The movements exercised there hold work to expand our imagination and, for this work, possibilities of emancipation.

Dance is also communal and culturally produced. In Afro-diasporic culture, dance is a form of knowledge production, literally sharing information to another through movement. Dance in dialogue with music may be productive in expanding our social imagination around an activist concept like "utopia" and how we might relate that to Janet's arc toward emancipation. The late scholar José Esteban Muñoz's (1967–2013) work on utopia emerges during the height of the visibility of the HIV/AIDS crisis in the United States. The Cuban-born, New York–based scholar was a critical figure in performance and queer studies, crafting art and theories around notions of national and communal belonging in his work. Muñoz's theories on utopia, as originated in response to HIV/AIDS in the 1980s and 1990s, were not meant as a way of escaping the impact of the virus, but a way to continue imagining a future for the body in spite of the virus. He was interested in producing alternative images and narratives to the overwhelming negative discourse on HIV/AIDS. Utopia for Muñoz centered a vocabulary of imaging what can and perhaps *will be* in the present sense.[4]

To argue for utopia, or emancipation, is a way to introduce the necessity of imagination to our political consciousness. We need to be able to envision that there will be a future for us, our elders, and those we have lost (our ancestors, foremothers, and forefathers before us) in order to politically organize against a system that wants to and is feverishly fighting to stifle that imagination. Activism on the dance floor (be that in your room or in a club) has long been a doorway to tapping into one's sociopolitical consciousness. Scholar Herukhuti reminds us that "you have to engage in grassroots organizing in your own bedroom to change the culture."[5]

The grassroots organization that emerges in one's bedroom has the potential to manifest itself in the streets and in the social arena. The Clit Club was a foundational lesbian bar in New York City, with primary headquarters on the corner of West 14th street and Washington Street from 1990 through 2002. It was one of the few lesbian and queer spaces in New York City that was multiracial from the start.[6] The work of Clit Club founders Jaguar Mary and Julie Tolentino points to these activist practices that center the interpersonal connections and possibilities that can be found on a dancefloor.

In addition, this club advocated for gender inclusive terminology and provided educational pamphlets around the HIV/AIDS virus. The space of the club gave individuals not only a much-needed night out (as Janet's "Go Deep" entails) but also an opportunity to learn, organize, mobilize, and mourn those lost to HIV/AIDS. The dance floor in Clit Club and elsewhere can channel that possibility for engagement with others while expanding our day-to-day movement to imagine something else for your body, be that love, mobility, or care. Raising imaginative alternatives of what could exist for your body in an environment where your body is facing real harm was precisely what dance floor activism is trying to produce. It is helpful to view this practice in dialogue with the emancipation that Janet draws out for those lost to the virus in "Together Again."

"Together Again"

Released as the album's second single on December 2, 1997, "Together Again" became Janet's eighth number one single on the Billboard charts. Amid the mixed feedback on the album, "Together Again" was consistently praised as a standout. The disco-inspired song is homage to the numerous friends of Janet that passed away from complications of HIV/AIDS. The mournful celebratory track was originally crafted to be a ballad before Jam, Lewis, and Jackson decided to take a page out of disco history and turn that ballad into an anthem. In so doing, they were able to draw out the emancipatory possibilities the song conveys through the capacity to dance *with* the ghost of a lost friend.

Letting go of the pain to hold onto the memory is the song's argument and one that is foreshadowed by the "Interlude: Memory." Memory in "Together Again" moves the body, emotionally and physically. Memory, like Sankofa, when harnessed, has the ability to push us toward a utopia of what *could* exist—rather than what does—with those lost. The strength of "Together Again" is its belief that memory creates possibility for ways of living and mourning. It is a way of keeping the ghosts of our loved ones, or pasts, alive within us.

There were two other mixes that gained popularity beyond the disco mix for "Together Again." The first is the "Deeper Mix" that retains and draws out the ballad foundation of the song. The other is the "DJ Premier 100 in a 50 Mix," which, like the Timberland/Missy mixes for "Go Deep," draws out Janet's interest in club and hip-hop sonics. The "Deeper Mix" features a music video shot by Renée Elizondo Jr. In the video, Janet appears in an apartment mournfully passing time. Her hennaed red hair is straightened. She wears a black spaghetti strap dress as she sings and reminisces her lost loved ones.

Toward the end of the video a CGI butterfly emerges and begins to shadow Janet before landing on her hand. Janet has stated that the butterfly was the manifestation of the love and light of her friends that she can carry with her.

The "DJ Premier Mix" is less known but is my all-time favorite remix of a Janet Jackson song. DJ Premier has long been considered one of if not the best hip-hop producers of our generation. DJ Premier in the late 1990s was working with leading hip-hop artists Mobb Deep, Mos Def, and the Notorious B.I.G among countless others. DJ Premier's addition to "Together Again" further sonically locates Janet as part of growing hip-hop community, if not, among the best of them. She performed the "DJ Premier Mix" at the 1998 American Music Awards on January 26. The version features heavy bass and cymbal beats along with prominent beatboxing throughout. The "DJ Premier Mix" is a completely different song and is very reflective of hip-hop music in the late 1990s, laid back and smooth. Remixes keep a song's structure, its potential open and fluid to be revised, reworked, and remade again. Remixes also invite fans to participate in reworking the song. If someone else can change it, why not you?

The move toward disco for the main album mix was an inspired one. Janet stated that she wanted the song to sound reminiscent of the original disco diva Donna Summer and her hit single "Last Dance." Although not sampled in "Together Again," the two songs use disco's rhythmic magnitude to produce joy and movement in releasing the tension of pain, heartache, longing, and sorrow. Janet is reminded of her youth, hanging out with Michael at Studio 54 at the age of ten. The memories of inclusion, excess, and joy projected by individuals who society deemed "freaks" are what Janet remembers for "to be included was to be loved."[7] Studio 54 has long been remembered for its hedonism, but what may be sidelined is how it crafted a place for queer inclusivity with no judgment, a place that Janet manifests on "Together Again." It is not a stretch to imagine that the feelings of inclusion from hanging out with Michael and LaToya at Studio 54 bled over to fashion *The Velvet Rope*. "Together Again" can be viewed as the *other* space of inclusion that Janet hopes to arrive to, a space where many of her friends already exist—"Dancin in moonlight/I know you are free."

Again, freedom is introduced as an alternative space to internal or structural oppression of the album. Yes, *The Velvet Rope* builds toward reconciliation, but the crux of the album is its potential for freedom. Each of Janet's expressions of freedom on the album carry an explicit sociopolitical connotation. "Free Xone" expresses freedom in opposition to homophobia, "Rope Burn" expresses a sexual freedom through consent, and "What About" expresses a freedom from the past and an abusive relationship. Elsewhere, the singer argues freedom from one's self. In "Together Again," the freedom is linked to remembrance that restores those lost to HIV/AIDS but also emancipation from a system that did not and could not care for them. Make no mistake, the devastating amount of individuals lost to HIV/AIDS in the 1980s and 1990s was due to a complex intersection of legislative failure and the lack of care produced by racism, sexism, homophobia, and transphobia. While the visible height of the crisis may have passed, HIV/AIDS has only risen in communities of color, specifically Black in the United States and disproportionately affecting Black women.

"Together Again" makes its political call for emancipation clear through its dedication as opposed to its lyrics. Lyrically, the song makes no explicit reference to HIV/AIDS and yet there has never been a period in my life where I did not know that this song was about a loved one lost to the virus and all those lost to it as well. Janet was vocal about its meaning from the beginning. The song's connection to HIV/AIDs came up in every interview, review, and discussion of the album. In the album's liner notes her dedication to those lost to the virus is the most detailed and explicit. "I dedicate the song "Together Again" to the friends I've lost to AIDS, Dominic, George, Derek, Bobby, Dominic, Victor . . . José. I miss you and we will be together again. This was written for you."[8]

The song's promotional material is the symbol for solidarity of people living with HIV/AIDS. I cannot overstate the importance of Janet openly mourning friends lost to complications from HIV/AIDS in 1997. Her mourning was contextualized as a loss from the virus at a time in which family members were still silencing loved loss to the virus by omitting their struggle after one's death.[9] By taking this mourning song public, she was not only sharing her grief but making their deaths, socially available to a larger public as opposed to one that remained hidden and silenced. There was no shame to be had in "Together Again," just joy and a declaration for freedom from being condemned to live without the right to a life.

The Remedy of Poetry

In the "Interlude: Sad," Janet muses on the overwhelming nature of depression in that you can have everything and still feel depressed. She teaches listeners to water their spiritual gardens in order to remain afloat in the struggle. There are several threads running in this short interlude. The first is the recognition of deep depression outside of socioeconomical struggle. Due the paucity of discussion around mental health in society, we collectively attribute most forms of depression as the result of some type of conflict and assume that things will be better once that conflict is alleviated. When Janet entered the studio in 1996 after signing the largest record deal ever granted to an artist, she found herself recognizing her depression as its own entity and not one that was tied to a specific battle.

We may have Sigmund Freud to blame for depression or melancholy being understood as some form of lack. Freud theorized that the difference between mourning and melancholia is the attachment to an object in that when you are mourning the object/person is lost and so after a time that loss is understood in relationship to the object/person.[10] Whereas melancholy is the perpetual state of mourning an object loss in which the origins are unclear, just producing a sense of loss. In the Showtime docuseries on Rick Rubin's studio *Shangri-La* (2019–present), Rubin offered some pointed commentary about depression and capital that artists bring with them and try to work out in the studio. The production of music in that space of emotional lack is pursued with the belief that it will fill or replace something,

"Most people who are really driven for something are doing it because they think it's going to satisfy something in them. Yet often, most worldly things tend to not be so satisfying."[11] In this assertion, we can see how the widespread belief that depression is something that can be physically replaced or filled can often be unproductive when pursuing spiritual or emotional healing.

Janet's interlude speaks to the real crisis of her depression while pointing to a cultural practice of watering her spiritual garden as a remedy. The lyric brings to mind the work of Alice Walker where she reminds Black women to be in search of their mothers' gardens as a way to hold onto memory in their lives for spiritual guidance.[12] Walker's statement argues for Black women to look for the creative work produced by your mother, by those unseen women in history as the practices they enacted to survive will be your tools for survival and will keep their memories and labor alive. "Interlude: Sad" expresses to its audience that there are other ways of being/ feeling/knowing in this world that are not represented to Black women in history and may need to be conjured up by turning to the past to make sense of the unnamed women before us, including ourselves. The ways of being/feeling/ knowing that exist in Black feminist circles or womanist positions work through the genealogical memories of our foremothers to assess our spiritual needs in the present.

Alice Walker's book of poetry *Revolutionary Petunias* navigates the impossible quest for revolution while affirming the need to create, make, and hold onto beauty in times of strife. This beauty is not a person but rather exists in the arts/ poetry to manifest your life into a poetic form.[13] *The Velvet*

Rope becomes more productive when placed in dialogue with the larger historical practices of Black women's narrative literary practices and the blues. To be sure, Janet is doing something different but to give *The Velvet Rope* a genealogy is to suggest that what she was experiencing was not new, not different, and not an aberration. Her need to water her spiritual garden is a historical art form that Black women have always turned to by way of exorcising their demons and their woes in a society that does not want to hear them.

"Special"/ "Can't Be Stopped"

"Special" hears Janet talking with a friend and sharing the difficulties that she has endured over the past few years. She talks about crying during the day and shares her experiences to affirm the feelings of her friend, presumed to be similarly living with depression. Janet moves on to then declare the right to be special for everyone, including herself.

The song features a sense of optimism by having birds slowly chirp in the background. Additionally, it features backing vocals by the United Children's Choir, who assist in uplifting Janet's ode to reconciliation. "Special" argues for healing but recognizes the labor that goes into making healing a reality. Doubt rears its head in "Special" but Janet preserves her desire to move forward. In *True You*, she expressed her desire as an artist to not dwell or work in darkness, even when working through dark topics. Sankofa holds great wisdom here as its symbol makes time and memory fluid. To move forward you must deal with your past, "Because wherever you will run there you will be." Ultimately, Janet proclaims that watering your spiritual garden creates a space for emancipation. Reconciliation is not the end but it is a start toward envisioning emancipation from abuse for oneself and it is ultimately a *work in progress*. She states in her 1997 *Ebony* magazine interview that "I can honestly say that for the first time I really like myself. I really do. And now, I'm working at learning to love myself."[14]

Emancipation is not for the faint of heart. The opening track of an album introduces the theme solidified by the closing track, the "hidden" track "Can't Be Stopped." Until recently, the track was unlisted and appeared as part of the same run time on "Special." The "hidden" nature of the song suggests a desire to include its sociopolitical explicitness as part of the same narrative but one that exists as a coda as opposed to being part of the narrative itself.

"Can't Be Stopped" is a self-directed anthem from the singer to herself and a larger anthem about fighting back against injustice and oppression. The song is an intra-community conversation—the audience that Janet is speaking to is racialized as Black. This is heard in the declarative call-and-response structure of the song by referring to her audience "brother" and "sister," terms used to convey intra-cultural exchange between non-familial-related Black individuals. Janet reminds the audience to stay strong and that they come from a lineage of kings and queens when facing opposition. The kings and queens Janet may be referring to are the kingdoms of the Gold Coast Tribes (specifically what is now Ghana but also other parts of West Africa) that existed prior to the Portuguese settlements that landed in 1482 and ignited the Trans-Atlantic Slave Trade. The kingdom of Akan is part of that history and is the originator of the Sankofa symbol that Janet carries with her throughout the album on her body.

In the face of opposition and oppression, be they internal or social, "Can't Be Stopped" affirms the strength that the singer and her intended audience carry with them. She performs a practice of present-tense belonging through past affirmation, "Don't ever forget where you come from" is the most literal embodiment of Sankofa. The arc of *The Velvet Rope* is to provide the Janet and the listener with a future by giving them a history to work with in the present. The future set in motion by the artist affirms the personal and structural woes of Black women and other bodies at the margins. Experimentation through the album's aesthetics, sexuality, and performances pushes her body and the listeners into space to imagine and perform emancipation. Experimentation enables Janet to shed her history with respectability politics, and pushes her toward consciousness raising of more liberatory representations of her gender and race in the world. To follow the chanting crowd in "Free Xone," *Let's Get Free!*

6
Let Me Just Fuck with It for a Minute

Janet Jackson is one of the first MTV artists. Jimmy Jam acknowledged the immersive visual qualities available in Janet's music during her *MTV Icon* special in 2001. Janet's career emerged during the crossover period of the early to mid-1980s, where musicians were simultaneously becoming audio and visual artists. Post *Control*, she sets the template for utilizing music videos as an extension of the song's message as opposed to a mere reproduction or promotion for the song. Other artists of her era were radio stars prior and learned to adapt and work with music videos as they become more prominent. By centering Janet's simultaneity of the audio/visual in her work, I am not creating a comparison model to other artists in that era but rather aim to highlight Janet's innovation when it comes to co-crafting visual documents that challenged the landscape of artistic, cultural, and sociopolitical production. She received the Video Vanguard Award in 1990 based on the videos produced for *Control* and *Rhythm Nation 1814* alone and did not even include architecturally poetic "Love Will Never Do Without You" directed by Herb Ritts.

Music videos have served as an opportunity for Black entertainers to experiment with their identities and cultural histories since the late 1970s. Media scholar Carol Vernallis writes that music videos in the 1980s were *the* laboratory: "While commercials and films . . . tended toward tightly controlled client-author supervision and careful storyboarding, a music video director or editor might try anything."[1] Black artists may have been drawn to the medium's unrestricted supervision and policing, enabling them to craft documents where they could experiment with their representation, exercise mobility, and portray stories that otherwise would not be visible otherwise. Since the music video's audience was the home consumer and not the traditional modes of film distribution, there is an affordance provided to the artist in not having their body regulated or the content stifled if a producer does not think it will "sell." Black artists who have historically been regulated out of cinematic representation found music videos to be productive terrain for alternative representations of Black bodies not commonly seen onscreen.

The MTV origins of the production, promotion, and circulation of the music video may appear to be a dated history or of a bygone era to a contemporary music video audience. Many scholars have noted that while the history of the music video predates the invention of the television set, it was MTV who ushered the mainstream visibility of the music video in the early 1980s.[2] Although MTV initially suppressed its viewing of Black artists after much public ridicule and pressure from artists, they began screening videos by Black artists which would change the landscape of trajectory of the genre in the years to come.[3]

The music video's airplay offered potential for a "repeated performance that increasingly mirrors radio airplay due to media synergy. The formal and content of the music video—fashioned as performance and seduction—is layered to encourage multiple viewings as well."[4] This structure has contributed to the success and transformation of numerous Black artists including Prince, Michael, and Janet Jackson. In so doing, music videos, even amateur ones, have enabled the increased visual presence of Black bodies onscreen and has thus been used to challenge harmful stereotypes and affirm Black culture. Moreover, the laboratory nature of the medium also allowed artists to experiment with form. Many artists have used that space to collaborate with directors to push the form in new and exciting technologically progressive eras. Such music videos may challenge the very definition of what the cinematic is.

The videos for *The Velvet Rope* draw from the wealth of global Black diasporic culture (not just Black American culture) to reflect upon the expansive and quotidian, daily and mundane nature of Blackness as a site for continual possibility and emancipation. The audiovisual images created for *The Velvet Rope* capture Janet's desire to incorporate a specifically Black cultural practice and aesthetic in addition to ushering her viewers into critically examining the problem with Black women's representation in time. Likewise, Janet's collaboration with directors for *The Velvet Rope*'s music videos shows a desire to use technology to draw out bodily senses, memory, symbolism, and imagination. The totality of *The Velvet Rope* music videos introduced and popularized new forms of technology to produce a cinematically affective representation of Blackness.

"Got 'Til It's Gone"

Co-conceived by Janet and Mark Romanck with added design by hair stylist Janet Zeitoun, "Got 'Til It's Gone" opens with the camera panning over an assembled group of Black men and women gazing back at the viewer. The video then cuts to Janet wearing her hair in an assortment of twists rocking to and fro with the 808 drum beat as Joni Mitchell's voice comes in via a mixed sample. In the video, Janet is seen with minimal makeup and acts as a lounge singer in an apartheid South African bar. The video captures the raw sonic engagement of that which structures the entirety of the album.

Director Mark Romanek drew inspiration for the video from *Drum* magazine, a South African magazine targeted at Black South Africans, that documented life under apartheid. The magazine captures the multitude of ways in which Black Africans used photography as self-making practice from the 1950s through the 1980s. One of the magazine's most prominent photographers, Malick Sidbé stated that his photography was blissful, "There was always music and a nice atmosphere, not a hint of sadness. Since I didn't have to worry about fixing people's hair and posing them properly, I was able to create spontaneous images of joy—and in that sense, the party pictures were more interesting for me."[5] Sidbé's quote captures the ecstasy or the desire for ecstasy produced from a socio-economic condition of oppression and mourning, suggesting that in turmoil there is a possibility for celebration and pleasure to take place; this sentiment is perfectly captured in the video but is also structured in *The Velvet Rope* itself as Janet never loses sight of pleasure despite her pain.

Janet described the production of her videos as collaborative projects that draw out other dimensions of the songs' possibility. Romanek uses the photography of Sidbé, Seydou Kïta, and Samuel Fosso to recreate the portrait studio in the space of the lounge, enabling participants to stage their own bodies for representation. In between bright flash-bulb shots we see Janet singing to the audience as onlookers—unable to gather in the densely crowded dance floor—peer through a plexi-glass window. The video uses quick shots and edits to suggest an entire world is present in the space of the video: Q-Tip dancing among the audience, men using the urinals, flirtation, and an outdoor shower. The video feels both immersive and quick, constantly demanding us to rewind, replay, and reflect.[6]

The opening image sets up the stark contrast of pleasure and sweat present within the lounge as we see a crowd of Black faces demurely staring at the camera. The following scene shows exactly where this party exists within the "sacred" space of a "Europeans Only/Slegs Blankes" building. But there are no white individuals in this space and at the end when the beer bottle crashes against the sign we realize that this joyful kickback happened through an occupation of that space. Or, it could be a derelict building from apartheid that bears the visible sins of the past while revealing the "white" flight that has rendered this former whites only space devoid of its namesake. The setting and how the bodies came to occupy that space is ambiguous. It does not matter how the evening came to be. The memory and possible legislative oppressive power that produced and enforced that segregation is symbolically and physically still present in the video.

The television inside the lounge is the audience's glimpse of that outside space that Janet and company are escaping. We see the occasional ethnographic footage of the representation of Africans from the Dutch perspective. One clip shows a white woman fondling the hair of an African woman as she smiles at the camera. The setup of the portrait studio not only draws attention to the photographic staging found in *Drum* magazine but also signals to the power of producing meaning through images. We see the bodies in the space of the lounge experiment with movement, posing, and gesture to document some other type of representation not commonly seen on screen or in print. In this video, the camera gives power back to the people. The self-fashioning performances from the actors involved express the desire to control their representation and shows that it is not crafted solely by the director.

The South African setting of apartheid makes a visual argument to rethink what social imaginations of racial progress might look like. The setting critically reminds audiences of the temporal immediacy of apartheid as it had only been three years since its removal in South Africa. Janet, additionally, uses her body along with Q-Tip's to situate their

Black American nationality in that same structure, suggesting a diasporic practice of communal bonding, linking their present realities with the not-so-distant past of segregation. The apartheid setting expresses the need for pleasure in the space of the lounge amid a larger sociopolitical structure of oppression. The space of the club in the video presents a *loophole of retreat* for these bodies. Loophole of retreat refers to the attic that Harriet Jacobs hid in for seven years before escaping slavery. Black cultural theorists and artists have theorized Jacobs's loophole of retreat to refer to the temporary spaces that present relief, hiding, or growth for Black bodies who face oppression. It is theory that I find useful to describe the space of relief that is carved out through the video and as *The Velvet Rope*'s arch reveals, it builds a space for freedom.

"Together Again"

Light has long been utilized to represent a variety of symbolic meanings in society. In Renaissance paintings the use of light from an "unnatural" source in painting was meant to evoke the divine will of God or God's light. During the Enlightenment the representation of light was transformed to represent consciousness and intellect, and in the nineteenth century light represented technological progress and modernity. In our current era the use of light in art can stand in for any of these symbolic meanings. In "Together Again," light symbolically refers to all three.

In her book on the use of material excess, light, and embodiment in the Black Diaspora entitled *Shine: The Visual*

Economy of Light in the African Diasporic Aesthetic Practice,
Krista Thompson argues that light in many urban, working-
class Black communities operates as a technology of visibility
and value.[7] This is to say that light as articulated through
bling, cell phone flashlight, LED screen light, and the like
as seen in mall photos, dancehalls, and proms, is meant to
mirror the music video light that makes a star shine. This
low-tech recreation of video-light in daily Black life is not
only a manipulation of new forms of photographic and digital
technology but is also rooted in a social history around the
absence of light for Black bodies in visual work. Light in this
daily context draws inspiration from both the symbolic and
the technological in that the light around you not only pulls
you closer to the divine but literally makes you stand out.

"The idea of painting with light is now a reality," said
an infomercial for the Quantel Paintbox system released in
1990.[8] A predecessor to Photoshop, the Quantel Paintbox was
still rooted in digitizing analogue media and using analogue
media manipulations like photomontages, superimpositions,
fade outs, and so on. The possibility to paint with light, long
lusted after by visual artists, spearheaded a generation of
photographers and filmmakers to produce aesthetically rich
texts that prioritized the luminosity of the subject. It was now
possible to use a single light source or luminous spot in an
analogue image and spread that "natural" light elsewhere
to the image. This effect creates a hyperreal image in that
the content is from our reality but the light source is not.
Media makers now had "God"-like abilities through their
creative practices with Quantel Paintbox making their use of
light limitless. The Quantel Paintbox aesthetics possibilities

first emerged in photography before making its debut on television through music videos.

French fashion photographer Seb Janiak is a pioneer in the field of digital photography through analogue manipulation without digital cameras or printing. His work essentially laid the ground for the type of hyperrealistic photography and filmic content that dominates our media landscape today. His early photographic work with the Quantel Paintbox enabled him to produce the *Uchrony* series (1989–95).[9] *Uchrony* features architectural landscapes that forge a reality familiar yet foreign due to Janiak's use of photomontage and light manipulation. Opera Houses are "realistically" encased in abandoned buildings, the Statue of Liberty is perfectly broken apart in a downtown city corridor, a large naval ship appears in the middle of the city, and so on.

Janiak, his work still firmly rooted in reality, utilized emerging technology to expand on his practice in an effort to build worlds that imagine some spatial alternative to the world we are currently living in. His artistic oeuvre by the fall of 1997, which included a spectacular "alien" series photo shoot with Naomi Campbell, made him a leading candidate to direct Janet's "Together Again." If the song is about harnessing the light of a loved one, Janet needed someone who could harness, manipulate, and paint with light for the video.

I want to read the video for its technological use of light produced by superimposition and photomontage because reading light in this video allows us to comprehend the social narrative at play. I also want to steer away from readings that suggest the music video for "Together Again" is Afrofuturistic. It is not. Afrofuturism refers to a specific use of time manipulation in a Black culturally produced art product to point to time periods and locations, like Sun Ra's use of outer space, beyond oppression. "Together Again" does not point to another time nor spatial zone, but instead lifts the veil of this material world to crossover to the spiritual one to see her loved ones again. This is not to suggest that the narrative is at odds with Afrofuturism but rather to clarify that cultural terms crafted to refer to Black cultural production require specificity and are not deployable to all content produced by a Black body.

The video opens with a solitary and somewhat sorrowful Janet perched atop a rock overlooking a barren wasteland as she sings the opening verse of the song. A falcon appears by her side. As the beat kicks, the sorrowful video changes to an expression of joy and abundance. Gone is the barren landscape, now the land features a harvest, a rainforest, and is filled with a diverse array of people and wild animals coexisting alongside one another. Janet spends most of her time in this other world smiling, dancing, lounging with panthers, and cradling a version of herself who may have crossed over at some point. Janet dons similar extended twist-outs to the ones seen in the "Got 'Til It's Gone" video. She wears garments with some South and East African specificity while other individuals wear garments influenced by South Asian territories. Much like our world this other world is multicultural but the distinction is the explicit visibility of difference. "Together Again" is an idealized world, splendid with models and fashion to match and in that way is not reflective of our "reality."

The video's use of light is what carries its symbolic meaning to an audience. The world in "Together Again" is immaterial and the video executes that position by having it end abruptly, a lightning strike back to where it began, in the wasteland with a solitary Janet now overlooking an oncoming storm. The encroaching darkness represents the absence of light that makes up the singer's reality. During the second verse, we see Janet and company in a greenroom-like enclosure as they dance. The light in that space shines too bright to be naturally produced. When Janet sings the bridge in the song, the light becomes unbearable in that location and overwhelms her body receiving it.

The light comes from a source not of this earth and not available to the human eye. Technology, the video suggests, may make it visible for us to grasp the light of god. This vignette is rendered very similar to the "annunciation" style paintings of the Renaissance era where we see the Angel Gabriel deliver the proclamation of God's divine will to Mary (to bear Christ). Paintings of this era, specifically Jan van Eyck's *The Annunciation* (1434–6), used natural light to illuminate areas of "man." However, the light cast on Mary is not of this world and is often contradictory to the sun's patterns during the day. This is because the light on Mary is God's light shining directly upon her. This unnatural light alerts the audience of God's power to produce light (creation) and illuminate the spirit; it is *this* light that engulfs Janet from above in the video.

Elsewhere in the video, many of the subjects carry equal illumination in the large crowd/gathering scenes. Janiak uses superimposition to overlay or stitch together a crowd from multiple analogue shots. We can see this in the scene with the "two Janets" and large assembly with the animals in the background. The individuals featured in those shots all carry the lighting used in their original shots (the lighting needed to capture their features). In a group shot, there is only so much natural light or studio light available for all the subjects. Moreover, lighting across different skin tones can be particularly challenging to illuminate all subjects involved. Black skin has historically been poorly lit on screen because of racial biases, privileging white skin to take up an abundance of the available light. In a video featuring a large multiracial cast, the new technology of digital superimposition is able to retain the light of each individual and create a document where they are pictured alongside one another with equal luminosity. The symbolism of light here not only is powered by technology but allows us to view the light of the individual spirit, their consciousness. Light in "Together Again" plays upon classic symbolism alongside new technology to intervene in the act of creation reserved for a higher power. Janet and Janik use their creative power to lift the veil on her material world to envision that other space of freedom where her friends who have since passed from the HIV/AIDS exist in abundance.

My access to music videos pre "cable-access" fall of 1998 was largely dictated by visiting distant relatives who had cable, retail stores that would play videos on their monitors or at the music video kiosks that existed in trendy junior/teen shops at the mall like *Wet Seal*. These video kiosks were perhaps the most important as it gave me on demand access. I can fondly recall parking myself at the single kiosk for hours while other, actual teenager shoppers tsked furiously at the young girl mesmerized by the moving images and sounds beating through the thick headphones, baiting time while her older sister tried on jeans with her friends. On these mini-screens, one had the opportunity to play music videos from a variety of "Top 40" singles at the time. In some cases, artists would permit a single or two from their forthcoming/latest album to be played on that kiosk. It was at these kiosks where I was able to watch "Together Again," on a loop and meticulously follow the choreography. I would repeat the moves in my room later that evening, participating in my own bedroom dance activism of sorts.

Although I am a millennial, I sometimes feel that the "kids these days" or even members of my generation do not understand the cataclysmic shift that digital technology brought to accessing musical content, specifically music videos. While we can, and I often do, bemoan the way digital technology creates a lack of medium specificity with content, we cannot deny that it has made a variety of artistic content more accessible and affordable for people to engage with, something that was not true for individuals, like me, who were in the lower end of the socioeconomic spectrum in the late 1990s to early 2000s.

"I Get Lonely"

Directed by Paul Hunter, "I Get Lonely" acts as a travelogue extension of space, design, and sexual embodiment. The video is emblematic of other late 1990s Black R&B

aesthetics, where design and architecture were integral parts of developing and forging new expressions of Black culture. The Los Angeles–born Paul Hunter emerged during the renaissance of music videos in the mid-1990s. Hunter's visual aesthetics are very sleek and sharp, driving the sequential movements of the video clip. Hunter, who was largely employed by Black artists until the early to mid-2000s, gave his artists abstract narratives that enabled them to be action stars. Aaliyah's "One in a Million" has the singer ride off in the moonlight on the back of a motorcycle; Missy Elliot's "Hit Wm Wit Da Hee" has Elliot levitate and conjure ghouls in a graveyard; Mariah Carey's "Honey" famously plays the chanteause's fantasy of being a Bond girl. We might consider Janet in "I Get Lonely" as an action star as well, albeit one that propels the action with and through eroticism. In this video, eroticism is used to give the audience a foundation by which we move through space in a video that is void of narrative and heavy on abstracted shots and design.

The video opens with Janet en-route. We see shots of her gazing outside the window of a car to rainy streets. The camera zooms inside the car door hinge where a spatial unfolding appears to the viewer. In this minimalist white hallway, we see Janet canvassing the halls wearing a sleek Dior suit with push-up bra (in which one reviewer remarked gave a starring role to her cleavage). The unfolding shot to this other space lures audiences to consider that the music video contains worlds within worlds; there are loopholes available for Janet to routinely dive into to have time for desired reflection. In between these shots we see Janet on a steel rotunda dancing with her backup dancers who make a daring, iconic reveal by unbuttoning their white-collar shirts to reveal their bustiers. The choreography for the "ballad" single of the album highlights the fact that, unlike Janet's previous ballads, "I Get Lonely" is a mid-tempo R&B song and carries the possibility of movement to its groove; movement that is rendered stylistically possible by Tina Landon.

Janet and Hunter discussed building a world in the video where Janet would be traveling to some unknown better place not envisioned onscreen. The structure of travel runs dominant throughout the clip and tends to be a running theme in Hunter's work; "One in a Million" by Aaliyah, "Honey" by Mariah Carey, and Faith Evans's "I Get Lonely"–inspired "All Night Long" all feature the lead singers in motion traveling to some other destination. By having Janet traveling, the video presents an artist in a physical and emotional zone of stasis and suspense. Janet admits in a BBC featurette that "music is so visual" nowadays and that further she clarifies that a music video does not need to tell a story to get its point across, it can be just "shots." Music videos by the early 2000s began to submit to digital technology's ability to oversaturate videos with information and shots so that they can be images wafting around to sound. Paul Hunter's collaboration with Janet signposted that digital shift in the era of analogue video production.

Hunter directed both the single version of the video and the "TNT Remix" featuring Blackstreet. The versions are more or less similar with the exception that Blackstreet joins Janet in the main rotunda stage for their verse and to occasionally give "face" to the camera in between shots. Costing just over a million dollars, the ample budget for the video enabled an artistic view to be achieved without having to cut corners. Hunter tells the cameraman for the BBC "Making of" featurette that the arcs, hallways, large ceiling ornaments all have a futuristic feel to them and the design is meant to be sleek and modern. Janet and Hunter achieved this "futuristic" design by looking at an unspecified airport in Japan. The architecture and design in the "I Get Lonely" make the video *feel* modern.

If, according to architectural historian Beatriz Colomina, what makes modern architecture modern is its engagement with media and not its functionalism or the use of materials, we may want to view Hunter's work as an extension of architecture's twentieth-century turn to media production.[10] Modern architecture in music videos uses the spatial possibilities available to the medium to further link space to music. Design now has a soundtrack in the music video. Music videos starting in the 1990s stitch together architectural expansion by connecting buildings that are stylistically similar but spatially worlds away from one another in reality. The perfected cityscape of real-world architectural feats exists in music videos like "I Get Lonely." The perfected design of a city or space can be rendered possible through the editing hand, revealing expansive corridors lurking between every formal opening and shot.

Hunter and Janet design a liminal space for Janet that takes the artist traveling to happiness drafted by a technological bent without the evocation of technology per se. But, it also becomes a vessel for eroticism to be contained within it. The empty, aesthetically pleasing spaces alert our senses but do not hold them. Janet's body in that space, then, drives sequential movement between shots and sustains the audience's attention for the clip. The emphasis on Janet's body and its eroticism points to how cinema generates the senses (be that emotional, physical, or both). The camera recognizes our desire to *feel* her in order to make us feel *for* her. By drawing out the eroticism of the video, it accentuates the overwhelming sadness and isolation that Janet feels. Janet lures the camera in through her body but has nowhere to go *and* no one to go to. She and the viewer exist in between space.

"I Get Lonely" situates Janet's body as an uncontained erotic object.[11] We can see that emerge when Janet begins to undress a "male" mannequin in a series of tight shots focusing on her hands undoing buttons, caressing its silver chest, and her lips kissing its cheek (a similar but less steamy shot appears in Mary J. Blige's "Love is All We Need" also directed by Hunter). The sexiness of the video teases out "I Get Lonely's" narrative of overwhelming isolation to the point of self-gratification. This side of "I Get Lonely" is alluded to on when the song plays in the background while Janet masturbates on the album-cut "Speaker Phone." Much like "Got 'Til It's Gone" and "Together Again" before it, the video expands the metaphoric engagement of the album's arc and experiments with the music video's capacity for world building, imagining alternative spaces for the singer's body.

The creative, risky direction of *The Velvet Rope*'s music videos play a significant role in a larger body of mid- to late 1990s music videos that were credited to revitalizing the format. As Christopher John Farly writes in his *Time* magazine article "New Video Wizards," music videos hit a peak in 1991 and then began to drastically lose steam by 1995.[12] The innovative directors like David Fincher who were so essential to the production of the music video went on to produce "real" work in film. Music videos had reached an aesthetically creative dead end to the point where they were the butt of a Beavis and Butt-head joke in 1996. When MTV began listing the directors' credits at the beginning and end of the film, suddenly the format aesthetically opened up again. New directors like Paul Hunter, Floria Sigismondi, and Hype Williams emerged as aesthetic manipulators who could help artists get their audiovisual groove back.

Music video credits became evidence of a director's artistry to a larger audience. If your video was subpar you would be visibly credited for that subpar work but the pendulum could also swing the other way as well. If your video was aesthetically challenging, interesting, and innovative, then audiences could immediately cite you for your work bringing on other artistic opportunities. *The Velvet Rope*'s music videos divulge Janet's creative hand in the medium as well. Through her engagement with collaboration, the videos for the album are conceptually rich extensions of *The Velvet Rope*'s arch toward self-actualization. The videos are technologically innovative documents that push the medium's engagement with the representation of Black women, narrative, camera angles, symbolism, and the medium's origin as a promotional document, not just for selling the album but for selling the tour as well.

7
Welcome to My World

There's a velvet rope we have inside us, keeping others from knowing our feelings. . . . I'm trying to expose and explore those feelings. I'm inviting you inside my velvet rope.[1]
—*Janet Jackson*

The Stage Is Her Playground

A young girl dances frantically to music. The music stops, and a young boy asks the girl how she would convince her lover to stay in her life. Beat. The young girl sashays left to right and stands with her hand on her waist, hip akimbo. She purrs into the microphone, "Come here lover boy!" The audience erupts in thunderous applause at the Mae West impression, and a young Janet and Randy smile and continue to sing Mickey and Sylvia's "Love Is Strange." Not only did Janet work the stage but she made it work for her in that clip and in the forty-six years since. At the infamous 2009 MTV Video Music Video Awards audiences bore witness to a series of unforgettable moments that included a meandering Madonna spoken tribute to Michael Jackson (who among us can forget, "and so was I?"), Kanye West interrupting Taylor Swift's acceptance speech, and Beyoncé performing with hundred-plus background dancers for "Single Ladies," but it was Janet Jackson who stole the night with her ninety-second performance of "Scream."

There was sweat, tears, and possibly blood shed on that stage and in the audience. She channeled her emotions and used the dynamic structure of performance to work it out. Unlike Janet's earlier narratives on being taught to hide her emotions on stage, at the 2009 *MTV VMAs* she showed aggression, sorrow, and an attitude in that tribute. She reminded her critics and the audience through kinetic vigor, sharp choreography, expressive facies, a rolled neck, and a rolled eye to put some respect in her name. And they took notice. As Michael Slezak wrote for his *EW* review, "She worked that stage harder than an underpaid assistant doin' overtime, and as tributes go, this was as energetic as it was heartfelt."[2]

As a performer, Janet has always had to not only work the stage but work it harder than some of her contemporaries. The stage was the final frontier for Janet's albums and, along with the music videos, it extended the arguments, emotions, and narratives of the albums. Journalist David Ritz took notice of Janet's rigorous tour schedule and performance execution for his follow up to the "Joy of Sex" interview with the singer, entitled "Sex, Sadness, and Triumph" for *Rolling Stone*. Although *The Velvet Rope* did extremely well, it took longer for it to reach the same milestones that *janet.* did.

Much was riding on the tour doing well, not only to boost album sales but to "justify" *The Velvet Rope*'s existence. The opposition to the album meant that from the moment Janet hit the stage on April 16, 1998, in Rotterdam through its conclusion on January 30, 1999, in Honolulu, she had something to prove.[3]

Conceptually, *The Velvet Rope Tour* is an epilogue to the album. In her 1998 *Rolling Stone* interview with Ritz, Janet explained that for the first time she thought of key tour details before finishing the album. The tour would draw out those metaphors that were misunderstood to her audience. The tour utilized cutting-edge technology in dialogue with traditional cabaret and vaudeville styles to present an evening that worked the album out for audiences, forever changing the field. *The Velvet Rope Tour* would transform how pop stars toured their albums, namely with regard to the carnival/funhouse inspired set design (i.e., P!nk's *Funhouse Tour*, Britney Spears's *The Circus Tour*, and Christina Aguilera's *Back to Basics Tour* to name a few) and more critically with how the screen is used to displace the performance onstage. *The Velvet Rope Tour* was one of the first tours to incorporate an LED screen as a backdrop. This incorporation produced so much light that the lighting rig for the tour needed to center the screen and not the stage.[4] The effect of this decision produces a performance that is meant for the screen and not for the immediacy of the audience's eyes. Beyoncé's tours, specifically *The Formation Tour*, are a prime example by which we see this cinematic performance in full view. The way the "live" can be captured and remixed via the LED screen for the audience is the new experience of performance, and *The Velvet Rope Tour* was perhaps the first to do so.

"You": Commercial Edition

Janet executed strategic marketing skills for the tour, including using the music video for "You," her fifth single, as a promotional clip for the tour. Released in September 1998, the tour itself had already been in production for five months. The video, which utilizes footage captured from her show in Sweden, relies on soft light and focus to capture the illustrious glamour of the star and her performance. This music video is, *actually*, a commercial. It is noticeably less "raw" than the HBO taping of her performance at Madison Square Garden just a few months later, where we see Janet sweat, pant, and appear charged and emotionally overwhelmed. "You" is selling you something: an illusion of an experience that you would want to have for fear that you might be missing out.

The video opens with an array of visuals unfurling to the audience via the LED screen at the start of the show. The virtual screen doubles itself in the footage. The audience watches a LED screen projecting the image of the entertainer to a camera that projects that image through the screen of our television sets. This doubling heightens our experience with the image, an effect that video capitalizes on. We see a close-up of Janet wearing a white button-up shirt and a black-and-white striped vest with a black tie. She looks directly at the screen as she begins to sing the first verse of the song. Her black hair is slicked back into a high ponytail. A year after the album's release, Janet was beginning to shed the persona she developed and wore over the course of the album. Gone were the corkscrew curls, the septum piercing, and the red hair. The only evocation of that persona materializes in a single red streak that emerges from the ponytail that falls to her shoulders.

"You" carries the visuals from the tour as a way to have the spectacle and allure of the "live" travel to those who have yet to participate with the encounter just yet. It also served as a reminder of the spectacle for those who already had, in that they could point to this document and say, "I was there." The music video for "You" simultaneously exploits and dismisses the production of the live in that the commercial/video may be a better memory than the real thing, *and* the real thing is only something you can physically experience while Janet is in town. "Liveness," as Philip Auslander describes, works to unpack the media noise that is already present in live production, for the live event does not dismiss nor inherently negate the mediated version because it is live.[5] For "You," both iterations of the experience are necessary to capture the experience of *The Velvet Rope Tour*. Audiences want the "physicality" of being *there* as well as the stylized video that gives you unprecedented access to vignettes, close-up shots of Janet in soft focus lighting, Landon's meticulous choreography, and wardrobe changes not seen from your perspective. It is a video that exists beyond the space of the stage and gives fans playback control, intimacy, and on-demand access to a tour not just of a generation, if the video is to be believed, but of a lifetime.

Behind the Rope

A master of ceremonies pulls back the lush velvet curtains onstage. There is an enormously large book with the title *The Velvet Rope*. It opens. Inside the pages is an impressive LED screen. The then-new technology enabled a brightness to emerge from the screen, overpowering the stage lighting to center the visuals of the performance. Following the unveiling of the screen, we hear "Interlude: Memory" play over cosmic visuals featuring the Sankofa symbol. As the Sankofa symbol emerges from a burst of light, memory becomes twisted elegance. A blast of pyrotechnics is emitted from perimeters of the screen as it splits in two. *Ms. Jackson* descends from a crane at the top of the hidden staircase as the "Hobo Scratch" sample plays. Janet declares that we all have a velvet rope and invites us inside her for "we were all born with specialness inside of us. So tonight let love shine its light" before plunging into the "Velvet Rope."

The first section features Janet and her dancers dressed as nineteenth-century British merchants complete with oversized hats and stylish canes in costumes co-designed by Janet and David Cardona. In this opening block, Janet performs a series of choreography-heavy numbers, including "If." Throughout the evening, Janet would repeatedly end a routine by intensely staring out to the audience. Of these stares, none is more epic and "extra" than the one she delivered during the dénouement break for "If." After nailing the complex choreography for the song, Janet struts to the far left side of the stage as she sings the final leg of the chorus "Cuz I'm Not" she projects out to the crowd. Pause. Janet stares at her audience. Time passes. She continues to stare at the audience. Janet slowly unbuttons her Black tail coat while staring at the audience and the cameras for . . . four minutes (in the HBO airing of the show). She then exclaims, "If I was your girl!" before the stage lights cut to black.

The stare no doubt gave Janet time to catch her breath from the two previous energized performances, but it also gave her time to declare her authority over the space. What was the audience going to do during this stare, *not clap*? This was her show and the audience was here for it. The stare itself becomes a memorable way for female entertainers to make their presence known, not through movement, or through their vocality but by sheer presence alone. In the space of the performance, rarely do the performers break the proscenium arch to look back at us directly. To stare back is to recognize the presence of the audience and rupture the illusion. But Janet wants to break that illusion, and she does so to remind us that the stage is her world.

Following the completion of the first act, the stage transforms into a giant carnival outfitted with inflatable set designs by Mark Fisher. The frenzied feeling conveyed from the carnival vignette may represent Janet's relationship with escapism. This world is where she plays pretend but it is not a solution to her problems. After this fever dream has passed, Janet emerges in her New Jack Swing costume to perform "Alright" with a skyscraper skyline backdrop. Here, the screen is incorporated into the performance as a virtual casting of what is onstage by displaying the performance in a neo-noir augmented reality. At the conclusion of "Alright," Janet swaps her fedora for a bowler hat, removes her zoot suit coat; as the skyscraper skyline backdrop is dropped, a rippling green one appears in its place. She is about to break it down for "I Get Lonely." The performance incorporates choreography from the video, telling the audience "it's getting hot in here" and recreating the exaggerated unbuttoning black push-up bra reveal from the video. "I Get Lonely" transitions to the racy "Rope Burn," a performance that was so notorious it was used to sell the tour in the music video "You." The live performance of "Rope Burn" was advertised as a "can't miss feature" of the tour. Will *you* be the lucky fan to have your image onscreen? Will *you* be lucky enough to be touched by Janet? The only way to find out is to be there.

Janet was one of the first women entertainers to break the sacred/taboo barrier between being a fan's illicit dream and being a tangible object of their affection. *The Velvet Rope Tour* was not Janet's first use of audience participation; she first introduced it as a tactic during her *Janet World Tour*. During the audience engagement for that tour, Janet would dance for a male fan. One fan used that space to assault Janet.[6] She recalls being overpowered against her will by a male fan who kept rubbing her crotch. When Janet proposed the layout of *The Velvet Rope Tour* to her entourage, Landon was shocked that Janet wanted to invite a fan onstage again after the last tour. There would be a twist: the fan would be tied up. The restraints would make it difficult for any type of contact beyond what Janet laid out. By restraining the fans (with their consent) it allows for the singer to transverse the screen into their reality and the fantasy to play out for the audience. But, it crucially allows her to maintain control over the interaction and her body.

Janet flips the submissive role she plays on the album track through the performance. Here, the male audience member is the one who is gleefully being tied up while Janet is the one taunting her submissive. Janet along with Tina and Shawnette dance in front of and with a pole for the gentleman. On the HBO special for the tour, "Rope Burn" opens with a decoy.[7] The man assigned to be the submissive appears to be a little "too" prepared in his near sheer black scoop neck shirt and leather pants. Janet delivers a firm "no, try again." The dancers quickly do and pick an unassuming fan wearing a promotional tour shirt featuring Janet lounging on a chaise with a velvet rope binding her wrists. He begins to convulse, exclaiming gratitude every step of the way as Tina and Shawnette tie him down. And so began a long series of audience participation where Janet made the BDSM-inspired contraptions restraining the fans, culminating with the full-body harness she entrapped fans with on 2008's *Rock Witchu Tour*.

Janet concludes the tantalizing "Rope Burn" before channeling her inner rock god for "Black Cat" and the harrowing "What About." The audience is firmly on the other side of the velvet rope now. After a rousing performance of "Rhythm Nation" complete with nunchucks, Janet closes out the main arc of the show with "Special." As she sings, photographs of a young Janet emerge from the LED storybook screen behind her. It is a startling display of "happy" images that accompany a song detailing the immense isolation and unhappiness she felt growing up. They stun, insofar as the audience may realize that the family photo inherently is an artifice that masks the actual interpersonal dynamic of the home.

The family photos are often unable to document or account for abuse or unhappiness in the home. Janet's use of family photos unsettle the performance as the positive framing of these memories are questioned when the audience becomes aware of the emotional insecurity she felt behind these "happy" scenes. The LED screen that has hovered behind the singer was now lowered to encase her body with images. The performance ends with a portrait of a young Janet, with a one-sided ponytail and a half smile. Arriving on the other side of the singer's life is to confront that pain that she had been running from all her life. A vision of joy was just around the corner.

For the final leg of the performance, Janet returns to the stage wearing a more relaxed outfit compared to the stylized costumes seen thus far: a crop top and baggy pants. She sings, jumps, and grinds to hit after hit including "That's the Way Love Goes," "Got 'Til It's Gone," "Go Deep," and "Together Again." After a series of difficult performances the last section afforded a resolution for the tour and a moment of celebration for Janet and the dancers. For the HBO special, "Got 'Til It's Gone" received a cameo appearance by Q-Tip. The decision to screen the performance on HBO would mark a turning point for tour performances and their extended life beyond the stage and "liveness" of the moment. The HBO special for *The Velvet Rope Tour* created an archive for a Janet Jackson tour, especially as it was her first tour to be broadcasted in full on television in the United States. The special has found a second life online, where fans have copied and remixed key scenes from the performance to be played on repeat (including the classic "stare"). For some, watching the tour online is a reminder of what they experienced, while for others it is a way to imagine what a Janet tour (centering those songs) might feel like. For most of my adult life, the HBO special was my performance document of the album. I made peace with the fact that I may never see some of my favorite tracks from *The Velvet Rope* live. That was until 2017's *The State of the World Tour.*

Metamorphosis

On November 15, 2017, I sat in my seat at the Barclays Center in Brooklyn, New York, eager for Janet's *State of the World Tour* to begin. It would be my first time seeing Janet live. I was double fisting beers. I did not want to miss a second of her performance that evening, not even for a refill. Alone, I sat among a cluster of couples who seemed touched by my single-minded commitment to the evening. Before a single note began to play, a short video emerged onscreen condemning white supremacy. I immediately burst into tears. I figured I would cry at some point throughout the two-hour run time but I was surprised it happened so early in the evening. I was overwhelmed by Janet's attentiveness to sociopolitical issues, not shirking away from speaking out through her artistry. "State of the World" began with a song not played live since her 1989 *Rhythm Nation World Tour*. Ms. Jackson was fully present and informed us in that evening the need for imagining emancipation for all bodies is still on her mind. *Still.*

"State of the World" was not the only throwback track that evening. Janet performed "What About," last performed during *The Velvet Rope Tour*. She relied on a similar pantomimic choreography as the original performance. However, unlike *The Velvet Rope*–era performances, Janet does not open the song on her knees but remains standing throughout. In the original, Janet remained firmly outside of the pantomime with the exception of mimicking being violently struck down during the bridge.

In its revised performance, Janet physically intervenes in a vignette by pushing an abuser around. There were audible gasps in the audience. Tina Landon remarked that during *The Velvet Rope Tour*, "What About" was the performance in which she would really focus on the audience to gage their reactions. "There would be some nights in the middle of my performance . . . there's probably somebody here with their significant other standing behind them whose going through this right now. It's interesting because I could see women crying and the men behind them really uncomfortable."[8] These flashes of recognition of domestic abuse victims and their perpetrators in the audience would overwhelm Landon and leave her crying at the end of the performance. Landon wanted her choreography to remove the violence in those vignettes and not combat violence with more violence. She made a purposeful decision to feature the women taking care of each other and themselves as a turn to healing and reconciliation.

At the conclusion of "What About," Janet broke down in tears. She announced to the crowd, "You guys, this, this here is me." The pantomime of the proscenium arch was momentarily shattered. I had wept through every song for the performance, looked around, and saw a host of other attendees also sobbing. The allure of the entertainer is that they are above us, and we aspire to live their life. What makes the gossip of a celebrity's life so thrilling is the distance they hold in not confirming the speculation on their personal woes; we spend time wondering. Rarely, however, does an entertainer share that their body, in all its splendor, is not above the toxic ills of society. They too are still fighting and struggling with physical and emotional abuse from their partners, like many other individuals in the stadium. If *The Velvet Rope* was Janet's journey toward self-actualization from oppression then *The Velvet Rope Tour* was the beginning of Janet's interest in using the space of the stage to extend that process of self-actualization toward a collective emancipatory vision for her audience.

In May 2019, after twelve years of eligibility, Janet Jackson was finally inducted into the Rock and Roll Hall of Fame. When inducting Janet, entertainer Janelle Monáe expressed that she learned how to speak up about injustice by watching and listening to Janet. In her speech Janet thanked her constant companions, producers Jimmy Jam and Terry Lewis among a slew of others, but poignantly ended with a demand that the institution "induct more women." Janet's music has long been a form of teaching and expressing a sociopolitical conscience to a generation of Black girls and women. As I write this, Janet just wrapped her *Metamorphous* residency at MGM theaters in Las Vegas honoring thirty years of *Rhythm Nation 1814*, forty-six years after her breakthrough performance there of "Love Is Strange" with her brother Randy. The residency featured a slew of *The Velvet Rope* songs, and the album has been heralded in the twenty-plus years since its release for its experimental sound, bold vision, and strength in expressing her personal woes.

The Velvet Rope has impacted a generation of artists, thinkers, and writers around the world by affirming their realities, their pain, and making space for their personal issues to be political ones. The necessary unveiling of *The Velvet Rope* did not conclude Janet's journey toward self-actualization but set her apart from her contemporaries in her emotional vulnerability and affirmations of her struggles. It is an album/era in her life that has spoken truth to individuals', Black women specifically, struggles with abuse, isolation, trauma, depression, and sexual autonomy outside of heteronormative conditions. Through my headphones, Janet's work taught me how to imagine and conceptualize emancipation from the confined reality I had. The album carried me over from my restricted childhood and adolescent years to a road toward self-determination that has largely been a reality because I was inspired to speak from her music. *The Velvet Rope* gave me a voice and it made, and continues to make, my work and my life (along with so many others) possible.

Notes

Preface

1 Armando Garía, "Freedom as Praxis: Migdalia Cruz's Fur and the Emancipation of Caliban's Woman," *Modern Drama* 59, no. 3 (2016): 344.

Chapter 1

1 Angela Davis, *Blues Legacies and Black Feminism: Gertrude "MA" Rainey, Bessie Smith, and Billie Holiday* (New York: Vintage Books, 1998), xv.

2 Lisa B. Thompson, *Beyond the Black Lady: Sexuality and the New African American Middle Class* (Champaign: University of Illinois Press, 2009), 3.

3 Nicole Fleetwood, *On Racial Icons: Blackness and the Public Imagination* (New York: Routledge, 2015), 62.

4 Stephen Hold, "POP VIEW; Big Stars, Big Bucks, and the Big Gamble," *The New York Times*, March 1991.

5 Chuck Philips, "Janet Jackson Spins a New Record: $80-Million Deal," *Los Angeles Times*, January 1996.

6 John Norris, "Janet Jackson Discusses the Meaning of 'The Velvet Rope,' Pt. II," *MTV News*, October 1997, accessed September 1, 2019, http://www.mtv.com/news/1430424/jan et-jackson-discusses-the-meaning-of-the-velvet-rope-pt-ii/.

7 Laura B. Randolph, "Janet," *Ebony* magazine, December 1997, 158.

8 Danyel Smith, "Janet's Back: Miss Jackson Talks About the Pleasure in Pain—And Vice Versa," *Vibe* magazine, November 1997, 86.

9 Smith, "Janet's Back," 87.

10 David Ritz, "Sex, Sadness, and the Triumph of Janet Jackson," *Rolling Stone*, October 1998, accessed September 1, 2019, https://www.rollingstone.com/music/music-news/sex-sadness-an d-the-triumph-of-janet-jackson-108166/.

11 "Janet Jackson: The Making of 'I Get Lonely,'" *BBC TV Special* 1998, YouTube video, accessed September 1, 2019, https://ww w.youtube.com/watch?v=dyezLCGuwpY.

12 Janet Jackson and David Ritz, *True You: A Journey to Finding and Loving Yourself* (New York: Simon and Shuster, 2011), 124.

13 "Janet Jackson," *Fan de*, 1997, YouTube video, accessed September 1, 2019, https://www.youtube.com/watch?v=j8n AgH1socc.

14 "Janet Jackson," *Hey, Hey*, 1997, YouTube video, accessed September 1, 2019, https://www.youtube.com/watch?v=yOX lJLoTwKk.

15 "Janet Jackson Vh1 Fashion Award Speech and Interview," *VH1 Fashion Awards*, 1998, YouTube video, accessed September 1, 2019, https://www.youtube.com/watch?v=Ui-C_K43Jhs.

16 Cheryl Thompson, "Black Women, Beauty, and Hair as Matter of Being," *Women Studies* 38, no. 8 (2009): 832.

17 Thompson, "Black Women, Beauty, and Hair as Matter of Being," 840.

18 Oprah Winfrey, "Janet Jackson, *The Velvet Rope*," *Oprah Winfrey Show*, 1997, YouTube video, accessed September 1, 2019, https://www.youtube.com/watch?v=2ErgY5CUfho.

19 Jackson, *True You*, 107.

20 Jackson, *True You*, 127.

21 Karla F. C. Holloway, "Revision and (Re)membrance: A Theory of Literary Structures in Literature by African-American Women Writers," *Black American Literature Forum* 24, no. 4 (1990): 617–31.

Chapter 2

1 Sylvia Wynter, "We Must Learn to Sit Down Together and Talk About a Little Culture," *Jamaica Journal* 3, no. 1 (1969): 27–42, 39.

2 Smith, "Janet's Back," 90.

3 Jackson, *True You*, 31.

4 bell hooks, "A Feminist Challenge: Must We Call Every Woman a Sister?" in *Black Looks: Race and Representation* (New York: Routledge, [1992] 2016), 82–84.

5 hooks, "A Feminist Challenge," 85.

6 Robin Roberts, "Janet: Family Staged Drugged Interventions," *ABC News*, 2009, YouTube video, accessed September 1, 2019, https://www.youtube.com/watch?v=JdHj5Gn-2e4.

7 "Rhythm and the Blues," *Newsweek*, November 1997, accessed September 1, 2019, https://www.newsweek.com/rhythm-and -blues-171316.

8   Roberts, "Janet: Family Staged Drugged Interventions."

9   Toki Schalk Johnson, "Watch Your Manners," *Pittsburgh Courier*, February 3, 1951, 8.

10 "Janet Jackson," *MTV: Icon* 2001, YouTube video, accessed September 1, 2019, https://www.youtube.com/watch?v=-Uk Eg8Q9aww.

11 Kelly Alexander, "Janet Jackson's Velvet Rope 20th Anniversary: Tina Landon," *The Kelly Alexander Show*, November 2017, YouTube video, accessed September 1, 2019, https://www.youtube.com/watch?v=LHiMKy1iJpI.

12 Norris, "Janet Jackson Discusses the Meaning of 'The Velvet Rope,' Pt. II."

13 Randolph, "Janet," 160.

14 Audre Lorde, *Sister Outsider: Essays & Speeches by Audre Lorde* (New York: Crossing Press, [184] 2007), 62.

15 Smith, "Janet's Back," 85.

16 Jackson, *True You*, 124.

17 Jackson, *True You*, 25.

18 Jackson, *True You*, 56.

19 Jeanette Zinno, "I Had My First Colonic—Here's What I Learned," *Good House Keeping,* April 2016, accessed December 8, 2019, https://www.goodhousekeeping.com/beauty/a37909/first-colonic-experience/.

20 Ritz, "Sex, Sadness, and the Triumph of Janet Jackson."

21 Smith, "Janet's Back," 86.

22 Davis, *Blues Legacies and Black Feminism*, 55.

23 Davis, *Blues Legacies and Black Feminism*, 7.

24 Tressie Mcmillan Cottom, "Opinion: How We Make Black Girls Grow Up Too Fast," *The New York Times*, June 2017, accessed December 8, 2019, https://www.nytimes.com/2017/0 7/29/opinion/sunday/how-we-make-black-girls-grow-up-too -fast.html.

25 Janet Mock, *Redefining Realness: My Path to Womanhood, Identity, Love & So Much More* (New York: Atria Books, 2014), 143.

26 "Janet Jackson Talks About Unusual Tracks," *MTV News*, October 1997, accessed September 1, 2019, http://www.mtv. com/news/1430427/janet-jackson-talks-about-unusual-trac ks/.

Chapter 3

1 Danielle Butler, "'The Velvet Rope' Was a Challenging Record… My Conversation with Jimmy Jam," *Boombox,* October 2017, accessed September 1, 2019, https://theboom box.com/velvet-rope-was-a-challenging-record-my-convers ation-with-jimmy-jam/.

2 "Janet World Tour Special 1993, Part 1," *MTV*, YouTube video, accessed on September 1, 2019, https://www.youtube.com/w atch?v=ZOQKsLk99w8.

3 Frantz Fanon, *Black Skin, White Masks,* trans. Richard Philcox (New York: Grove Press, 2008), 8.

4 "Rhythm and the Blues," *Newsweek,* November 1997.

5 Jessica Hopper, "The Invisible Woman: A Conversation with Björk," *Pitchfork*, January 2015, accessed September 1, 2019,

https://pitchfork.com/features/interview/9582-the-invisible-
woman-a-conversation-with-bjork/.

6 Jim Farber, "True 'Velvet' Janet Jackson Gets Personal About
   Her New LP, Her Sexuality, and Her Famous Kin," *Daily News*,
   October 1998, accessed September 1, 2019, https://www.nyd
   ailynews.com/true-velvet-janet-jackson-personal-new-lp-
   sexuality-famous-kin-article-1.804955.

7 Various, *Joni Mitchell Tribute Compilation* (Promo), Reprise
   Records 1999, https://www.discogs.com/Various-Joni-Mitchell
   -Tribute-Compilation/release/3050935.

8 *Painting with Words and Music*, directed by Joan Tosoni
   (London: Eagle Rock Entertainment, 1998).

9 "Janet Jackson the Essential Interview," *MTV*, October 1997,
   YouTube video, accessed September 1, 2019, https://www.you
   tube.com/watch?v=F8jy5OJcmcI.

10 Butler, "'The Velvet Rope' Was a Challenging Record… My
    Conversation with Jimmy Jam."

11 John Berger, *Ways of Seeing* (New York: Penguin Books for
    Art), 148–49.

12 Sarah Jane Cervenak, *Wandering: Philosophical Performances
    of Racial and Sexual Freedom* (Dunham: Duke University
    Press, 2014).

13 Lorde, *Sister Outsider*, 62.

14 "Rhythm and the Blues," *Newsweek*, November 1997.

15 Jackson, *True You*, 125.

16 Jackson, *True You*, 125.

17 "Janet Jackson: The Making of 'I Get Lonely,'" *BBC TV Special*
    1998.

18 Jackson, *True You*, 27.

19 Jackson, *True You*, 4.

20 Butler, "'The Velvet Rope' Was a Challenging Record… My Conversation with Jimmy Jam."

21 Janet Jackson, *I Get Lonely*, Virgin Records 1998.

22 Jackson, *I Get Lonely*, 1998.

Chapter 4

1 "Janet and Lisa-Marie Speakerphone Interlude LMFAO," *Presley Jackson Board TapTalk*, August 2010, accessed September 1, 2019, https://www.tapatalk.com/groups/presleyj acksonfpb/janet-and-lisa-marie-speakerphone-interlude-l mfao-t799.html.

2 Janet Jackson, *The Velvet Rope*, Virgin Records 1997.

3 Rhonda Williams, "Living at the Crossroads: Explorations in Race, Nationality, Sexuality, and Gender," in *The House That Race Built: Black Americans, U.S. Terrain*, ed. Wahneema Lubiano (New York: Pantheon Books, 1997), 139.

4 Lorde, *Sister Outsider*, 139.

5 Lorde, *Sister Outsider*, 65.

6 L. H. Stallings, *Funk the Erotic: Transaesthetics and Black Sexual Cultures* (Chicago: University of Illinois Press, 2015), 60.

7 Viviane Namaste, *Sex Change, Social Change: Reflections on Identity, Institution, and Imperialism* (Toronto: Women's Press of Canada, 2011), 8.

8 Mock, *Redefining Realness*, 138.

9 John Norris, "Janet Jackson Discusses the Meaning of 'The Velvet Rope,' Pt. I," *MTV News*, October 1997, accessed

December 8, 2019, http://www.mtv.com/news/1430423/jan
et-jackson-discusses-the-meaning-of-the-velvet-rope-pt-i/.

10 Ernest Hardy, "The Velvet Rope," *Rolling Stone*, October 1997,
    accessed December 8, 2019, https://www.rollingstone.com/m
    usic/music-album-reviews/the-velvet-rope-195286/.

11 Stephen Thomas Erlewine, "The Velvet Rope Review,"
    AllMusic, 1997, accessed December 8, 2019, https://www.all
    music.com/album/the-velvet-rope-mw0000028459.

12 Daphne Brooks, "'All That You Can Leave Behind': Black
    Female Soul Singing and the Politics of Surrogation in the Age
    of Catastrophe," *Meridians: Feminism, Race, Transnationalism*
    8, no. 1 (2007): 187.

13 Norris, "Janet Jackson Discusses the Meaning of 'The Velvet
    Rope,' Pt. II."

14 Yashair Ali, "Exclusive: Les Moonves Was Obsessed with
    Ruining Janet Jackson's Career, Sources Say," *Huffington Post*,
    September 2019, accessed September 1, 2019, https://www.huf
    fpost.com/entry/les-moonves-janet-jackson-career_n_5b91
    9b8ce4b0511db3e0a269.

15 Shayne Lee, *Erotic Revolutionaries: Black Women, Sexuality, and
    Popular Culture* (Lanham, MD: Hamilton Books, 2010), 15.

16 Nicole R. Fleetwood, *Troubling Vision: Performance, Visuality,
    and Blackness* (Chicago: University of Chicago Press, 2011), 112.

17 Smith, "Janet's Back," 90.

18 Stalling, *Funk the Erotic*, 60.

19 Stalling, *Funk the Erotic*, 59.

20 David Ritz, "The Joy of Sex," *Rolling Stone*, September 1993,
    accessed September 1, 2019, https://www.rollingstone.com/m
    usic/music-news/janet-jackson-the-joy-of-sex-56099/.

21 Jackson, *True You*, 83.

22 Jackson, *True You*, 77.

Chapter 5

1 Kwami Coleman, "Mademoiselle Marby: Betty's Agency with and After Miles," *Betty Davis—They Say I'm Different Symposium,* May 2015, author's notes.

2 "Jenna Dewan Reveals That Janet Jackson Gave Her Vibrators," *Jimmy Kimmel, Live,* May 2018, YouTube video, accessed September 1, 2019, https://www.youtube.com/watch?v=jxW AZG0gdYE.

3 "*ALTERNATE ENDINGS/RADICAL BEGINNINGS,*" *Visual Aids*, December 2017, accessed September 1, 2019, https://vi sualaids.org/projects/alternate-endings-radical-beginnings.

4 José Esteban Muñoz, "Ghosts of Public Sex: Utopian Longings, Queer Memories," in *Policing Public Sex: Queer Politics and the Future of AIDS Activism*, ed. Dangerous Bedfellows (New York: South End Press, 2008), 356.

5 Herukhuti, *Conjuring Black Funk: Notes on Culture, Sexuality, and Spirituality* (New York: Vintage Entity Press, 2007), 24.

6 "The Clit Club Crew on the Clit Club for the 6th Annual Last Address Tribute Walk," *Visual AIDS,* July 2019, accessed September 1, 2019, https://visualaids.org/blog/the-clit-clu b-crew.

7 Jackson, *True You*, 60.

8 Jackson, *The Velvet Rope*, Virgin Records.

9 Sheryl Gay Stolberg, "Epidemic of Silence: A Special Report.; Eyes Shut, Black America Is Being Ravaged by AIDS," *The New*

York Times, June 1998, accessed December 8, 2019, https://www.nytimes.com/1998/06/29/us/epidemic-silence-special-report-eyes-shut-black-america-being-ravaged-aids.html.

10 Sigmund Freud, "Mourning and Melancholia," in *The Complete Psychological Works of Sigmund Freud,* ed. Anna Freud and trans. James Strachey (London: Hogarth Press, 1953–74), 243.

11 "Belief," *Shangri-La*, directed by Jeff Malmberg (Los Angeles: Tremolo Productions/Showtime Networks, 2019).

12 Alice Walker, *In Search of Our Mothers' Gardens: Womanist Prose* (Boston: Mariner Books, 2003).

13 Alice Walker, *Revolutionary Petunias: Poetry* (New York: A Harvest/Harcourt Brace Jovanovich Publishers, 1973).

14 Randolph, "Janet," 162.

Chapter 6

1 Carol Vernallis, *Unruly Media: YouTube, Music Video and the New Digital Cinema* (Oxford: Oxford University Press, 2013), 5.

2 Aisha Durham, "Check on It: Beyoncé, Southern Booty, and Black Femininities in Music Video," *Feminist Media Studies* 12, no. 1 (2012): 37.

3 Rob Tannenbaum and Craig Marks, *I Want My MTV: The Uncensored Story of the Music Video Revolution* (New York: Plume, 2011), 168.

4 Durham, "Check on It," 38.

5 Ellen C. Caldwell, "The Lasting Power of Janet Jackson's 'Got 'Til It's Gone,'" *JSTOR Daily*, October 2017, accessed

September 1, 2019, https://daily.jstor.org/the-lasting-power-of-janet-jacksons-got-til-its-gone/.

6 Vernallis, *Unruly Media*, 94.

7 Krista Thompson, *Shine: The Visual Economy of Light in the African Diasporic Aesthetic Practice* (Durham: Duke University Press, 2015).

8 "Quantel Paintbox Demo 1990," YouTube video, accessed September 1, 2019, https://www.youtube.com/watch?v=BwO 4LP0wLbY.

9 Angie Kordic, "An Artist, A Photographer, A Curious Mind— In Conversation with Seb Janiak," *Widewalls*, November 2017, accessed September 1, 2019, https://www.widewalls.ch/photo grapher-seb-janiak-interview/.

10 Beatriz Colomina, *Privacy and Publicity: Modern Architecture as Mass Media* (Cambridge, MA: MIT Press, 1994).

11 Lee, *Erotic Revolutionaries*, 13.

12 Christopher John Farley, "The New Video Wizards," *Time Magazine*, 1997, accessed September 1, 2019, http://content. time.com/time/magazine/article/0,9171,138232,00.html.

Chapter 7

1 *Janet Jackson, The Velvet Rope Tour: Live in Concert*, directed by David Mallet (London: Eagle Rock Entertainment, 1999).

2 Michael Slezak, "Janet Jackson Single-Handedly Saves MTV VMA Tribute to Michael Jackson," *Entertainment Weekly*, September 2009, accessed September 1, 2019, https://ew.com/article/2009/09/14/janet-jackson-michael-jackson-vmas-2009/.

3 Ritz, "Sex, Sadness, and the Triumph of Janet Jackson."

4 Janet Jackson, "On Set of the Velvet Rope Tour," *BET*, 1998, YouTube video, accessed December 8, 2019, https://www.you tube.com/watch?v=pfWLJN26tQk.

5 Philip Auslander, *Liveness: Performance in a Mediatized Culture* (New York: Routledge, 1999), 3.

6 Jane Stevenson, "CANOE—JAM!—Action Jackson," *Toronto Sun,* 1998.

7 *Janet Jackson, The Velvet Rope Tour: Live in Concert.*

8 Alexander, "Janet Jackson's Velvet Rope 20th Anniversary: Tina Landon."

Also Available in the Series